EUROPE OF THE CATHEDRALS

GEORGES DUBY

MEDIEVAL ART

EUROPE OF THE CATHEDRALS

1140 - 1280

BOOKKING
international

Georges
DUBY

II. MEDIEVAL ART
Europe of the Cathedrals
1140-1280

First published in 1966-1967

© 1995 by Editions d'Art Albert Skira S.A., Geneva

Printed in Switzerland by
IRL Imprimeries Réunies Lausanne s.a.

Library of Congress Cataloging-in-Publication Data

Duby, Georges.
    History of medieval art, 980-1440

1. Art, Medieval.   2. Cathedrals.   3. Christian
art and symbolism—Medieval, 500-1500.   4. Civilization,
Medieval. I. Title
N5970.D798   1986   70902   85-43525
ISBN 2-605-00301-9

CONTENTS

THE ART OF FRANCE

The meaning of the term "cathedral" is a bishop's church, containing his *cathedra* or throne, and since this was always located in a city, the art of the European cathedrals reflects the revival of urban life that took place in the twelfth and thirteenth centuries. During that period towns grew steadily larger and wealthier, proliferated their suburbs along the main roads and, north of the Alps, became the chief centers of the most advanced culture of the time. But they drew their vitality almost entirely from the neighboring countryside. Many noblemen preferred town to country life and it was to the towns that the produce of their domains was carted; hence the ever increasing prosperity of the merchants trading in wheat, wool and wine. The town owed its affluence to the country and, by the same token, the art of the cathedrals thrived on the wealth of the rural areas, and it was brought to fruition, if indirectly, by the labors of innumerable peasants, wheat and vine growers, builders of dikes and watercourses, who exploited indefatigably the resources of the soil. That plenteous crops and prolific vineyards lay at the origin of the towers of the noble cathedral of Laon was frankly recognized by the architects when they placed at the summit the effigies of plough-oxen, and on the capitals clusters of vineshoots. Similarly the cycle of the seasons was represented on the façades of the cathedrals of Amiens and Paris by images of rustic labors. A well-earned tribute, for it was that peasant sharpening his scythe, and those others planting and layering vines whose humble toil gave rise to the great churches. Throughout the period the new zest for intensive husbandry was nowhere more pronounced than in northwestern Gaul, and the most fertile regions of the world were brought into full production in the plains surrounding Paris. This is why the art which now arose was commonly described as "the art of France." It came to its full flowering in the province which then bore this name, where Clovis had died and which lay between Chartres and Soissons, its seminal center being the city of Paris.

First city of medieval Europe to become a real—and royal—capital (which Rome had long ceased to be), Paris was in fact the capital not of an empire, nor of Christendom, but of a realm, the Kingdom of France. The urban art which matured in Paris under the forms we now call Gothic was an essentially royal art, and its leading themes celebrate a sovereignty, that of Christ and the Virgin. For in the Europe of the Cathedrals the power of the kings was gaining ground, freeing itself from the shackles of the feudal system. Before formulating, for his church of Saint-Denis, the rules of his new aesthetic, Abbot Suger had built up in the service of the Capetians the image of a suzerain king, apex of a hierarchical pyramid, vested with and concentrating all the powers that had hitherto been dispersed among the feudal overlords. Of all the States then in process of reconstruction, the largest and best organized was the kingdom whose monarch had his seat in the city of Paris. Throughout Latin Christendom no other ruler had more renown and wealth than Louis IX (St Louis). And this wealth flowed in through all the channels provided by seignorial dues and the financial obligations of vassalage, levies on cultivated land and vineyards.

Moreover Louis IX, a deeply religious man, did not regard his function as being merely temporal and secular; he felt himself, and wished, to be above all a faithful servant of the Church. From Joinville's *Histoire de Saint Louis* we learn how, after a light-hearted youth, St Louis decided to forsake all worldly vanities, "to love God with all his heart," and to do his best to live as his friends the Franciscans told him Christ had lived. Fifty years earlier much of the wealth of the richest monarchs, such men as Henry II of England and Richard Cœur de Lion, had been squandered on mundane pleasures and the recreations of the knightly caste. To the mind of St Louis, austerity befitted the King of France whom the rite of coronation had made the Lord's Anointed, and in a sense an avatar of Christ.

Had it not given him the miraculous power of healing sick men by the laying on of hands and an equal place among the bishops consecrated with the same rites? Thus the king devoted his wealth to the service of God, to works of piety, and built not palaces but churches. True, like the bishops, St Louis clad himself on occasion in fine raiment, but he did not adorn his residences and in the whole tenor of his life observed a strict simplicity. When administering justice he sat under an oaktree at Vincennes or on a terrace. It was he, rather than the German emperors, who inherited the fabled glory of Charlemagne, theme of the medieval verse chronicles. When, again like Charlemagne, he drew freely on the royal treasury for the building of a chapel, he was following in the footsteps of his ancestors who by reason of their lavish donations to the bishops, could rank as the true builders of the new cathedrals that had sprung up in France.

Sponsored as it was by royal patronage, the art of France was basically liturgical; though it is known to have included non-religious works, these were of a minor, perishable nature and none of them has survived. Its major forms were devised by a small group of wealthy prelates in direct contact with the king, a group that represented, on the intellectual level, the most advanced thinking of the day. Holding positions of the highest rank in the feudal hierarchy, the bishops (and the canons who shared with them the worldly goods of Mother Church) owned the best lands and enormous barns which the tithes exacted at each harvest filled to repletion. They levied taxes on urban fairs and markets and part of the profits from trade and agriculture found its way into their coffers. The other part went to the lay nobility, much of it being absorbed by the festivals which bulked so large in the age of chivalry. But the nobility, mindful of their immortal souls, also made substantial offerings to God, that is to say to his representatives on earth. Moreover the social order of the time was so constructed that peasants and middle class were expected and enjoined to deliver a large part of their earnings to the military and ecclesiastical authorities. The poor were systematically kept on the brink of destitution, the wealth accruing from the development of agriculture was used to provide for the luxury of a favored few, and crowning the pyramidal structure of the State was the king who, conscious of being himself a priest, was surrounded by bishops when he made his deci-

sions. In short the French cathedrals, an apanage of royalty, were an outcome of the new prosperity of the countryside.

Under the auspices of a stable and enlightened monarchy the art of France acquired a fine serenity and little by little sculptors mastered the expression of the smile, token of a new-found joy in life. And since the sacred and the secular were combined in the *persona* of the king, the temporal entering into a mystical conjunction with the eternal, this joy was not only of a mundane order. The art of the cathedrals culminated in the celebration of a God incarnate, in figurations of an inviolable union between the Creator and his creatures. It sublimated to a transcendent plane and, so to speak, sacralized the careless rapture of a young knight galloping across the flower-strewn fields of May and trampling down light-heartedly the growing crops.

But it would be a mistake to read into the moral climate of the thirteenth century the serene joy expressed in the faces of the crowned Virgins and smiling angels. For life was hard, not to say barbarous. It was an age of storm and stress, ravaged by internecine conflicts and social unrest. The bishop of Laon who planned the new cathedral could not forget that his predecessor had been brutally massacred in a revolt of the townsfolk. In 1233, infuriated by the exactions of another prelate, also a cathedral builder, the citizens of Reims rose up against him, forced him to close down the workyards for a time and to dismiss the masons and sculptors in his service. Such troubles were only incidental and sporadic. But they throw light on the latent fissures in the structure of the feudal social order, firmly established though it was. In it three groups were constantly at odds: the priesthood, the nobility, and the oppressed, exploited, submerged masses. For even the knights were in conflict with the Church, with its rigid moral code, with everything that tended to restrict the free exercise of their favorite activities: fighting and lovemaking. And artistic creation, too, was hampered by this nexus of conflicting purposes.

Still, there is no denying the relative stability of this social system in the period from 1140 to 1280. The "underground" movements which gradually modified its structure hardly affected the closed circle of clerics which commissioned artists and directed building operations, and in practice had little effect on the process of artistic creation itself. Its evolution coincided, by and large, with the progress of religious thought. We have, then, to give more attention to the theology than to the sociology of the period if we wish to understand its art.

During this phase of European history, marked by a steady increase in production and commercial activity, men's minds were the prey of conflicting emotions: on the one hand an urge for amassing wealth and profiting by the new prosperity, and, on the other, an idealization of the life of poverty and chastity enjoined on the true Christian as the surest means to the salvation of his immortal soul. In this age, when the great European kingdoms were taking form, there was another problem that weighed heavily on the minds of the Christian community: which of the two establishments spiritual and temporal—Pope or Emperor, Church or King—should wield sovereign power and regulate the conduct of society. And both these conflicts tended to merge into a wider, more fundamental issue, the antagonism between orthodox faith and the deviations of heresy. A prime concern of every bishop and, soon, of every monarch, was to combat the "false prophets," to refute their arguments and to hound down their sectaries. An equally urgent need was felt to rid the Christian faith of the uncertainties of its early, prelogical phase, to formulate a comprehensive, clear-cut body of doctrine, to make its tenets known and acceptable to the public at large, and by demonstrating the fallacies of heresy to lead back to the fold all who had strayed from the Christian's proper path. The outbreaks of heresy so frequent at this time were symptomatic of the growing pains of Western culture as a whole—hence their violence. During the twelfth and thirteenth centuries an awareness of the prevalence and perils of heresy played a leading part in the development of an art that claimed to be an exposition of the truth.

No portraits were made in this period. It costs an effort to discern behind the Angel's smile a reminiscence of the drunkard's leer, the hollow cheeks of the mendicant, the set lips of the inquisitor. None the less these elements are latent under the mask of ritual serenity. Gothic statuary aimed at presenting an ideal image of man made perfect. But we must never forget that the men of the time lived in a world where brutality and rapine were the order of the day: also that the rest of Europe was far from accepting in their entirety the canons of Gothic art. For the Western world was still divided up into watertight compartments, and many regions stubbornly refused to conform to a program initiated in France and enacted by French kings. Attempts were made to enforce it in certain provinces, but there were always marginal areas of resistance in outlying regions. When we seek to ascertain the true relations between the early manifestations of a new creative art, the structure of the social order and the prevailing climate of opinion, we must never lose sight of this geographical factor. For the horizons of European civilization were greatly modified in the years between 1140 and 1280. Not as the result of a gradual mutation, but by leaps and bounds. Here chronology acquires a determinant value. In this essay we propose to chart the successive stages (and also the permanent elements) of the various forces which confronted and reacted on each other throughout this period.

I

GOD IS LIGHT

1140-1190

UPPER FRONT OF THE PORTABLE ALTAR OF STAVELOT: SCENES FROM THE LIFE OF CHRIST, ABOUT 1175.
MUSÉES ROYAUX D'ART ET D'HISTOIRE, BRUSSELS.

SAINT-DENIS

In 1140 the most royal of churches was not a cathedral but an abbey: Saint-Denis-en-France. After the reign of Dagobert, Clovis's successors chose this sanctuary to be the royal mausoleum and the three dynasties which ruled successively the kingdom of the Franks used it as their burial place. Charles Martel, Pepin the Short and Charles the Bald were interred in the royal vault beside Hugh Capet, his ancestors the dukes of France and his descendants the Capetian kings. Compared with Saint-Denis and its series of royal tombs, Aix-la-Chapelle (Aachen) plays a secondary, not to say adventitious role in the annals of European royalty. It was in the crypt of Saint-Denis that the genealogical tree of the French monarchy, which Clovis had founded with God's aid in virtue of his baptism, had its roots and there, beside the tombs of their forbears, that successive kings of France laid their crowns and the emblems of their power. It was there, too, that they went to take the oriflamme (the sacred banner of red and yellow silk) before starting on their campaigns; there that they prayed for victory, there that the chronicles of their exploits were recorded. This "master abbey" figured prominently in the legends of medieval France and furnished many of the themes of the epic *chansons* which, centering on the heroic figure of Charlemagne, hymned the praises of *la douce France*, her monarchs and their deeds. Thanks to royal benefactions, the abbey became extremely wealthy. It had control of the great Parisian vineland and the big annual Foire du Lendit, where the Seine boatmen loaded casks of wine for export to England and Flanders. That on the brink of the twelfth century its wealth was constantly increasing was due to the rising prosperity of trade and agriculture, and its prestige, too, increased along with that of the kings in Paris. On Saint-Denis converged that slow movement which had been gradually orienting the driving forces of Christianity away from the Empire, which the Ottos had reintegrated in Germany, towards the kingdom of the fleur-de-lys. Neustria was

having its revenge on Teutonic hegemony. Taken over by the Capetians, the Carolingian tradition reverted here, beside the tombs of Dagobert and Charles the Bald, to its place of origin, the true "land of the Franks," i.e. the plain of France (not Franconia). And the new art that came to birth at Saint-Denis clearly demonstrated this reversion.

It was due to the efforts of a single man, Abbot Suger. Though born of poor parents, he was a schoolfellow of the king and thanks to their lifelong friendship rose to a position of great eminence. On his appointment as abbot of Saint-Denis, he gave deep thought to the symbolic values of the abbey of which he was in charge. He saw in his post an honor of the highest order calling for the pomp and dignity befitting it. For he was a Benedictine, and his conception of the monastic way of life did not involve any idea of poverty or withdrawal from temporal affairs. Suger kept to the Cluniac path and, like St Hugh of Cluny, believed that the office of abbot ranked high in the terrestrial hierarchy and that it was his duty to embellish Saint-Denis by all the means in his power, for the greater glory of God. "Everyone is entitled to his own opinion," he wrote. "Personally I deem it right and proper that all that is most valuable should be employed, exclusively, to celebrate the Holy Eucharist. If golden pouring vessels, golden phials, little golden mortars were used, according to the word of God and at the Prophet's bidding, to collect the blood of goats and calves and red heifers, how much more must golden vessels, precious stones, and whatever is most valued among created things, be laid out with continual reverence and full devotion for the reception of the blood of Christ! True, there are some who disagree and say that all that is needed for this celebration of the Eucharist is a saintly mind, a pure heart; and we, too, explicitly affirm that it is these that chiefly matter. But we maintain that we must do homage also through the outer ornaments of sacred vessels, more particularly in the service of the Holy Sacrifice;

that the purity of their content may be seconded by noble exteriors." With these "noble exteriors" in mind, Suger devoted the great wealth of his abbey to creating a magnificent setting for the services taking place in it. In the period 1135-1144, despite violent opposition from the partisans of "total poverty," he rebuilt and adorned the abbey church. He was working, he declared, for the honor of God and the kings of France, the dead kings who were his guests and the living king, his friend and benefactor. Proud of his achievement, he described it at length in his *Liber de rebus in administratione sua gestis* and its supplement, *Libellus de consecratione ecclesiae S. Dionysii*. From these we gather that he saw this royal monument as a synthesis of all the aesthetic innovations he had admired in the course of his travels in southern Gaul. But he also wished to excel them and aimed at creating something new, at bringing Aquitanian and Burgundian procedures into line with the imperial, Carolingian, truly Frankish tradition. With this in view he imported into Neustria the Austrasian aesthetic and the sophisticated artistry of Aix-la-Chapelle and the Meuse region, and fused them into the Romanesque art which had made a bid to replace them. But it was above all as an *œuvre théologique*—a sermon in stone—that he envisaged the rebuilt abbey. And, naturally, the theology he had in mind was that of St Denis (Dionysius), the abbey's patron saint, first Christian martyr in the land of France.

The kings of France were buried near the earliest tomb in the royal abbey, that of the martyred saint, the Apostle of the Gauls. Suger and all his monks, like the abbots who had preceded him, identified this heroic missionary with St Paul's disciple, Dionysius the Areopagite mentioned in the Acts of the Apostles, reputedly the author of several treatises on Christian mysticism which had an enormous influence on medieval thought. Actually, however, these famous books, which were devoutly preserved in the royal monastery, were written by an unknown author in the very early Middle Ages. In 758 the pope had presented a Dionysius manuscript to Pepin the Short, King of the Franks, who had been educated at Saint-Denis; next, in 807, Louis the Pious, emperor of the West, was given a second copy by the East Roman emperor, Michael the Stammerer. The original Greek text of the works of the Pseudo-Areopagite was translated into Latin by Hilduin, an abbot of Saint-Denis,

and from now on the *Theologia Mystica* was closely studied at Saint-Denis, notably by Suger who derived all his ideas from it. Dante assigned a high place in the *Paradiso* (XXVIII) to

> Dionysius [who] with so great desire
> To contemplate these Orders set himself,
> He named them and distinguished them as I do.
> (Translation by H. W. Longfellow)

For the texts attributed to Dionysius (*Concerning the Celestial Hierarchy*, *Concerning Ecclesiastical Hierarchy*) present the universe as a structure whose orders are disposed in a precise hieratical gradation. Suger clearly derived his conception of the social order with the king at its apex from these writings. Basic to the teaching of Dionysius is the principle: God is Light. Of this initial Light, uncreated and creative, every creature has a share. He receives and reflects the divine illumination according to his capacity, that is to say according to the place assigned him in the scale of things and the level to which the ultimate divine Source has appointed him. Born of the *vera lux* of Godhead, the universe is one vast field of light, streaming down from that Source which gives each created thing its being and its place in the universal hierarchy. This light pervades the whole material universe, visible and invisible, binds all the orders of existence together in their Maker's love and, since every object reflects light to some extent, this "first radiance" starts a chain of reflections that, after striking down into the heart of darkness, sets up a counterflow of light, returning to its Source. Thus the primal act of Creation—"let there be light"—called forth *per se* a reciprocal upward motion towards the invisible and ineffable Being from whom all proceeds. Everything reverts to Him, using as stepping stones those visible things which at successive levels of the hierarchy reflect better and better His transcendent light. The created ascends to the Uncreated by a ladder of analogies and concordances. Each rung of this ladder brings man a step nearer to an apprehension of God and a perception of that superessential light which is more or less veiled in every earthbound creature in so far as it is refractory to His illumination. Yet every created being reveals to some extent, proportionate to its love of the Creator, the spark of light within it. Here we have the key to that "new art," the art of France, of which Suger's church is the perfect paradigm: an art of clarity, of progressive illumination. "The dull mind rises to truth through that which is material. And, seeing the light, is resurrected from its former submersion." Suger had these lines inscribed on the portal of his church, to act as an initiation and explain its function.

Suger began work with the porch. Built in the Carolingian tradition and including portions of the ancient basilica, this part of the earlier church still gives an impression of massiveness and gloom. One reason for this is that it stands for the first stage of the Christian's journey out of darkness towards the light. Another, that it befitted the entrance of the royal monastery to produce an effect not only of compelling power and regal majesty, but also of military efficiency, since in those days the king was primarily a war lord—an effect that is heightened by two crenellated towers included in the façade. None the less these towers are pierced by a series of arches and the light of the setting sun enters the interior of the edifice through the three portals, above one of which is a rose window facing west, first of its kind in any Christian church. Its light falls on the three lofty chapels dedicated to the celestial hierarchy, to the Virgin, St Michael and the angels. On the forefront of his church Suger gave visible form to his theology and created what was to be the prototype of the façades of the cathedrals of the West.

But it is in the new transparent choir that we find the greatest aesthetic innovation. Here, at the far end of the church, terminal point of the liturgical progress towards the rising sun, he installed a source of light untrammelled, a dazzling approach to the divine presence, by doing away with walls. With this in mind he bade his master-mason exploit all the architectural possibilities of what had hitherto been no more than a crossing composed of pointed vaults. Thus between 1140 and 1144 there arose "a series of chapels set out in a semicircle, thanks to which the whole church was flooded with an all-pervasive light pouring through marvelously translucent windows." In the early twelfth century it was found necessary to provide abbey churches with a great number of chapels. These were needed because every monk now held the rank of priest and was called on to celebrate daily masses. The plan of an ambulatory equipped with radiating niches had already been employed in Romanesque churches and Suger applied himself to making these niches pervious to light. This he did by modifying the structure of the vaults in order to open out bays,

and by replacing long stretches of walls with columns; this enabled him to realize his dream of imposing unity on the liturgical ceremony, by means of omnipresent light. All the worshippers were gathered together so as to form a united body both by their semicircle and, above all, by the unifying illumination. When this was implemented by a simultaneity of gestures, the effect was that of an unanimous celebration—a symphony of prayer. On the day of the consecration of the choir the Mass was solemnized "in such a festal atmosphere, in a manner so joyous and so corporate, that their euphonious singing, with its concord and harmonious unity, composed a sort of symphony more angelic than human."

Here we may see the influence of Dionysius, who particularly insisted on the unity of the universe. From the choir to the entrance of the church no obstacle impeded the flow of light which, filling the whole interior, converted the church into a symbol of the process of Creation. Suger dismantled the old roodscreen which "dark as a wall had cut across the nave, so as to prevent the beauty and splendor of the church from being obscured by any such impediment." Every barrier is laid low, everything that might halt the flux and reflux of the divine effulgence. "Once the new rear part is joined to the part in front/ The church shines with its middle part made bright/ For bright is that which is brightly coupled with the bright/And bright the noble edifice which is pervaded with this new light."

Suger had begun by making additions to both ends of the church. Time failed him to build between the porch and choir the nave uniting them, but we know that he had made plans for this. Adapting the new technique of vault construction to the traditions of Neustrian architecture, he envisaged it as a set of wide, continuous aisles, an anticipation in fact of the plan brought to fruition a century later at Bourges.

The mystique of light implicit in Suger's theological writings and the aesthetic deriving from it were not applied solely to the domain of architecture. For, to the thinking of the ecclesiastics of the twelfth century, there existed also certain objects in which the spirit of the divine was immanent and which could act as stimuli of mystical meditation. Like the subjacent plan of the sacred edifice, they invited the soul to proceed from the created to the uncreated, from things material to things ineffable. Such a power resided in certain precious stones to which mystical thinkers assigned peculiar properties, seeing in them symbols of the virtues which help the soul of man to elevate itself towards the ultimate Perfection. Basing their conclusions on certain passages in the Bible, they pictured the heavenly Jerusalem, destined to be the abode of "just men made perfect" in the fullness of time, as glittering with jewels. When Louis VII laid the first stone of the choir of Saint-Denis, he was given a handful of gems to lay beside it, while the clergy chanted "Thy walls are built of precious stones." Hence the practice of placing objects resplendent with jewels in the central portion of the church, their scintillations kindled by the light which, streaming through the bays, converged towards the choir, focal point of the sacramental rite. The prevailing taste for translucent substances, for enamels and jewelry (which in the past had fascinated the barbarian chieftains) found a justification, both mystical and liturgical, in the precincts of the altar. For, as Suger said, "when my whole soul is steeped in the enchantment of the beauty of the House of God, when the charm of many-colored gems leads me to reflect, transmuting things that are material into the immaterial, on the diversity of the holy virtues, I have a feeling that I am really dwelling in some strange region of the universe which neither exists entirely in the slime of the earth, nor entirely in the purity of Heaven; and that by God's grace I can be transported from this inferior to that higher world in an anagogical [i.e. upward-leading] manner."

In extolling the mediative virtues of finely wrought sacred vessels and jewels, the abbot of Saint-Denis was conforming to a tradition handed down by the great mystics of monasticism. But the special emphasis on light in the doctrine of Dionysius led Suger to assign to it a more precise, more vital function in the ordering of his church. It was in the "illuminated core of the edifice," at the transept crossing, that "the reliquaries of saints adorned with gold and precious stones" were placed "for contemplation by all who visited the church." Thus the basilica ceased to be what until now the Romanesque churches had been—merely a superstructure above a hypogeum or martyrium, an underground crypt to which pilgrims descended: a cellar-like place of awe-inspiring darkness where they had

but glimpses of the holy bodies in the dim religious light of tapers. In Saint-Denis the sacred relics were translated from their cavernous abode and its atmosphere of numinous awe, and brought up into the church itself. Among the reliquaries exposed to the full light of day that of St Denis, flashing with gems, held pride of place in the heart of an uninterrupted light, the very light of his theology. Itself a reflection, mirror of God, it contributed to the illumination of the assembled congregation.

The main altar already had a gold frontal presented by the Emperor Charles the Bald. Suger added three more panels "for it to be resplendent on all sides" and set forth around it the precious vessels belonging to the abbey treasure. "We adapted to the service of the altar a porphyry vase admirably fashioned by the sculptor's and the polisher's hand, converting it from the amphora it was formerly into a vessel shaped like an eagle, adorned with gold and silver. We acquired a precious chalice wrought of a single block of sard, and another vessel of the same substance but not of the same shape, which resembled an amphora, and yet another vessel seemingly of beryl or crystal." Clearly Suger had a fondness for rare substances, their broken gleams and swirls of lambent light, and employed a team of expert craftsmen on giving a functional value to these "collector's pieces." Assisted by "a strange miracle that the Lord vouchsafed us," he gave the finishing touch to his work by setting up in the heart of the church and visible on all sides a cross twenty-one feet high. "I had to stop work owing to the lack of precious stones and had not the means of procuring enough since their rarity made them very costly. Then, lo and behold, from three abbeys of two Orders, from Cîteaux, from another abbey of the same Order, and from Fontevrault, there came certain holy monks who entered our little room beside the church and asked us to buy a store of jewels—amethysts, emeralds and topazes—such as I could not have hoped to gather in ten years." (In those monasteries an ascetic interpretation of the Benedictine rule prevailed, more stress being laid on poverty, and the monks refrained from ornamenting their churches.) "They had been given these stones," Suger continues, "as alms by Count Thibaud. Freed from the need for searching for precious stones, I rendered thanks to God. We gave the monks four hundred livres (though the jewels were worth much more), and not only these but many other gems and pearls enabled us to give our church an adornment befitting so holy a place. I remember using some eighty marks of pure refined gold. We employed goldsmiths from Lorraine, sometimes five, sometimes seven, on making the pedestal adorned with the four Evangelists and the column on which stands the holy, delicately enameled image and the story of our Saviour, with all the allegorical figures of the Old Covenant set forth and, crowning all, the death of Our Lord on the topmost capital."

The Great Cross was placed near the altar frontal, a Carolingian work. Suger's feeling for style led him to avoid any discrepancies between the older work and the new. This is why he summoned artificers from the Carolingian province where the old art of the Empire still survived. And by so doing he introduced into the heart of Neustria the aesthetic traditions of Austrasia. At the very time when, to glorify the Capetians, Saint-Denis was welcoming and celebrating the saga of Charlemagne, Suger linked up this artistic heritage with the royal abbey he was creating, and thus speeded up and amplified the cultural mutation of which he was the originator. For the imperial, humanist "renaissance," charged with allusions to antiquity, which was promoted by the Lorrainese craftsmen, was poles apart from the aesthetic of the Cluniac monasteries, whose abstract signs, strange animals and far-fetched imagery it rigorously excluded. It exalted plastic values and gave a central place to the human element in its vision of the world.

When, after radically changing the prevailing idea of architecture by using it to promote a "theology of light," Suger restored, beside the tombs of Pepin the Short and Charles Martel, the forms employed by Carolingian artists for the glorification of their monarchs, he was associating himself with the second "renaissance" of which the regions around the Loire and the Seine were then the seminal center, and with the return to classical prototypes which was then being promoted by the admirers of Ovid, Statius and Virgil, by men like Hildebert of Labardin and John of Salisbury. Associating Charlemagne with his celebration of the triumph of the Capetians, Suger also drew inspiration from the Ada Gospel Book, the Hildesheim gates and the ivories of Reims. In a word, he imposed on the art of France its other specific—anti-Romanesque—traits.

To begin with, in the stained glass he ordered for his "more luminous" windows. Here we have, in fact, a transposition of Mosan enamels and a derivative of the Lorrainese and Rhenish innovations. So disposed as to enrich the light of heaven, to give it glints of amethyst and ruby and "to guide blind spirits into the paths of anagogical meditation," Suger's windows, like Ottonian lectionaries, like Mosan enameled altars and the mosaic pavements of antiquity, framed the human figure in medallions, isolated by successive cloisons. Thus he completely separated it from the architectural context in which Romanesque *imagiers* had deliberately imprisoned it. Suger decided to apply this same procedure, taken over from the goldsmiths and miniature painters of the ninth century, also to monumental statuary. In Burgundy and the Poitiers region he had seen portals adorned with sculptured figures in the façades of abbey churches. He imitated these, and to him were due the first great effigies in stone north of the Loire. In the porch of Saint-Denis, however, these figures flanked bronze doors (those of the Ottonian basilicas) and the modeling of the stone jambs had to be adapted to that of the metal. The result was that here the carved figures did not grow out of the wall like efflorescences of the masonry, but, being separated by a recess and a canopy (like those we see in Carolingian ivories) from the building itself, produce the effect of independent works of art. Displayed in this manner, like pieces from a cathedral treasure or goldsmith's work, the Wise Virgins of Saint-Denis were the first "framed" statues in medieval art. All these images, those in the porch and stained-glass windows, those on the golden cross and those of the treasure around it—all alike bear witness to the central fact of Suger's theology: the Incarnation. "Whoever you may be, if you seek to do honor to these doors, praise not the gold nor the cost of them, but the work and the art. Surely the noble work shines, but that which shines is its nobility; it enlightens men's minds and by these lights guides them to the true light whereunto Christ is the true door." At Saint-Denis the treasures of the world were assembled to glorify the Eucharist; it was by the grace of Christ that man entered the holy light filling the church. This "new art" created by Suger was a celebration of the Son of Man.

Romanesque artists had not disregarded Jesus, but they saw in him God, the Lord. They were still dazzled by the blinding splendor of the Burning

Bush and the apocalyptic visions of the Book of Revelation. But the Christ of Saint-Denis was the Christ of the Gospels, in the likeness of man. For Saint-Denis was built in the mood of exaltation following the conquest of the Holy Land. All the epic chronicles whose themes took form in the regions around the abbey conceive of Charlemagne as a crusader faring to Jerusalem; King Louis VII, too, went on a crusade soon after the completion of the Saint-Denis choir, and instructed Suger to act as his regent during his absence. In the half-century following the deliverance of the Sepulchre of Christ, when hosts of Christians made the pilgrimage to the Holy Land almost every year, all religious-minded churchmen, noblemen, even peasants, were intensely aware of the call of the East, of the places where Christ had lived and suffered, and they shared in that splendid hope which led the Neustrian chivalry and the king of France, earthly representative of the crowned Christ, to embark on the great adventure. A supreme achievement of the crusade was the concrete, conclusive discovery at Bethlehem of the Well of the Woman of Samaria and on the Mount of Olives of the human reality of the Saviour. Around the workyards of Saint-Denis returned crusaders talked of the Holy Sepulchre, and in this context the relics of the Passion, a nail from the Cross, a fragment of the crown of thorns presented by Charles the Bald to the abbey, acquired a profounder actuality. This is why Suger's theology shows a consistent attempt to link up the new image of God, the living Christ of the Gospels, with the old image of the Lord God which till then had dominated monastic thought.

Suger based his theology on principles resembling those which had obtained for several generations in the monasteries of the West and it took the form of an interpretation or "gloss" of Holy Writ. In the ninth century Walafrid Strabo had compiled his *Glosa*, a Biblical exegesis which all monks of a scholarly turn of mind had heard read or copied out for their own use. Starting out from the premise that man is composed of three principles, body, soul and spirit, Walafrid inferred that every verse of the Bible had three significances: literal, moral and mystical. All the intellectual activities of monastic writers were henceforth directed to elucidating the Scriptures on these lines. St Augustine, too, had written that "the Old Testament is but the New

Testament covered with a veil, and the New but the Old Testament unveiled." He held that the life-story of mankind fell into two phases, separated by the birth of Christ. The whole course of Jewish history was to be regarded as a prophetic series of events, in which Christian history was prefigured symbolically. Thus the Old Testament narrative contained a record of premonitory happenings having a spiritual significance whose true purport, St Augustine says, "is to be looked for in reality itself not merely in the words." The New Testament is the decisive, definitive history, adumbrated by the Old, which, though anterior to the truth—the new revelation—is not a cause but an effect of it. Christ "fulfils" the protagonists of the Old Testament and supersedes them. Here we have the doctrinal background of Suger's theology. But he gave expression to it, not in writing, but in images generated by his tectonic handling of light. What he aimed at was to bring out the concordances and analogies between the Old Testament and the Gospels which for his contemporaries, the crusaders, had now become a living reality. Though the iconography of Saint-Denis keeps to the canons of Romanesque symbolism, it deflects them towards the personality of Christ.

These reminders of the correspondences between the Old and New Testaments begin on the very threshold of Saint-Denis, in the porch. Here the imagery also serves the function of a profession of faith, the true faith, and a repudiation of heretical deviations. The portal is triple and at its consecration three priests simultaneously performed the rites. It was a representation of the Trinity, whose image figures explicitly at the summit of the archivolt. For in point of fact the whole system of Dionysius the Areopagite centers on the theme of the Trinity, itself a symbol of the Creation, and moreover the mystery of the Trinity was one of the subjects most ardently discussed by theologians of the period. (Recently, in 1121, the synod of Soissons had condemned Abelard for an heretical interpretation of the Trinitarian dogma in his *De Trinitate*.) Nevertheless the imagery in the portal is tributary above all to the central figure of the Three Persons: Jesus "the true door." This is why for the first time the columns supporting the arches are given the form of statues—of the kings and queens of the Old Testament. Assembled as a triumphal escort celebrating the new age inaugurated by the Incarnation, these figures of the old dispensation body forth the royal lineage of Christ, Son of David—his prefigurations—and also his ancestors in the flesh, those through whom he participated in the created world, the world of men. And, finally, these figures serve yet another purpose as symbols and reminders of the glory of kinghood.

This theme recurs in the center of the church, on the Great Cross, a shining symbol of the Redeemer's victory over the powers of evil and the emblem the crusaders wore on their garments. The Cross served to refute the lurking doubts of men of little faith and challenged the undercover sectaries who denied that man could be redeemed by the death of an enfleshed man. It arraigned that notorious heresiarch Peter of Bruys who at this very time was making a holocaust of crucifixes at Saint-Gilles on the southern frontier of Gaul. It also demonstrated the "concordances" by juxtaposing in the sixty-eight scenes adorning it incidents in the life of Our Lord and their Old Testament prefigurations. The same lesson is conveyed by the stained-glass windows of the three chapels on the east of the church; that of the south chapel shows Moses, *novum testamentum in vetere*, that of the northern chapel, the Passion, *vetus testamentum in novo*, while that of the central chapel shows the Tree of Jesse which, figuring forth the genealogy of Mary, inserts Christ, the body of God, in a human family, "planting" him so to speak at the focal point of human history, in Time and in the flesh. One of the windows, which represents Christ crowning the New Covenant and stripping the veils from the Old, bears an inscription which might be said to epitomize Suger's theology: "What Moses veiled is unveiled by Christ's teaching." And pervading all these analogies we can see an evident desire to combat the temptations of a facile dualism and to signalize, not God's transcendence, but His Incarnation.

A tendency prevailed in ecclesiastical circles to divert attention from the Psalms, the Books of Kings and the Apocalypse towards the synoptic Gospels. So Suger was naturally led to emphasize the human side of Our Lord, to give the Virgin a central place in the iconography of the stained-glass

windows, to represent the Annunciation, the Visitation and the Nativity on the main altar, and to locate on one of the windows, framed by the tetramorph, not the image of God the Father as at Moissac, but Christ crucified. At Saint-Denis, as at Conques, the Last Judgment figures on the central tympanum of the portal, but here the imagery is based on the Gospel of St Matthew as well as on the Book of Revelation. The old men making music are relegated to the archivolt and give place to the Wise and Foolish Virgins—symbolizing those who are mindful of God and those who are forgetful. The arms of Christ are stretched out as if crucified and nearby are the instruments of the Passion, while beside him are the apostles, St John (perhaps) on his left and on his right the mediatrix, the Virgin. Thus the glorious event of the Last Day and the scene of Calvary revealed their profound identity, and we have here a clear allusion to the high hopes of the first crusaders, whose minds as they made their way to Golgotha were haunted by a vision of the heavenly Jerusalem bathed in apocalyptic light. Greatly daring, Suger had himself represented just below in the attitude of a donor—the proud gesture, doubtless, of a creator content with his work, but also a reminder of man's presence in the very heart of the Second Coming. For in Dionysius's *Hierarchies* did not even the humblest of men share in the universal immanence of the divine Light? The basilica of Saint-Denis stands for a form of Christianity no longer expressed solely in terms of liturgy and music, but also in those of a theology, a theology whose leitmotif is the Incarnation. This is why Suger's work opened up a new dimension, that of man illuminated by the *verum lumen*.

Situated at a crossroads on the edge of the plain just north of Paris, among workmen's huts and vineyards, Suger's abbey church benefited by its central position in a region of France then in the ascendant both economically and politically. Saint-Denis opened up a host of novel possibilities; all the "new art" of France derived from it. Let us now turn to the first cathedrals, which tended to rationalize its message, to the Cistercian monasteries, which stripped it of its outward splendor, and, lastly, to the heretical movement, which shut its eyes to it.

In the early medieval West a church or palace treasure was not regarded as a luxury but as an obligatory manifestation of power and prestige. It was right and fitting that the form of God and the bodies of saints and kings should be encircled with a blaze of gold and gems. Their luster and beauty made visible to everyone the glory emanating from these bodies and the aura of sanctity with which they were invested, elevating them above earthbound men and assuring the veneration of the populace. In the heart of darkest Europe, amid the forests and waste lands from which famished nomads equipped with rough wooden implements scratched a precarious livelihood, all the wealth of a semi-barbarous age was accumulated at certain favored points, in churches and shrines containing relics and in palaces.

At the bidding of prelates and princes highly skilled craftsmen, utilizing the most precious materials, created gorgeous adornments for altars and royal thrones, vying in delicacy and splendor with those rare objects which, produced in ancient times or in far lands having a high cultural level, had found their way into the hands of their employers. They were often called on to re-employ these "collector's pieces"—relics of Roman antiquity, intaglios, cameos, crystals fashioned in the Byzantine or Islamic East—and to assemble and mount them in the vessels used for divine service or at royal banquets. Their task was to make the adornments of the sacred.

The best of the workshops were the oldest, those which had served the empire of Charlemagne, then that of the Ottos. Since the empire styled itself Roman, it was desirable that the objects which proclaimed the glory of the vital center of Christendom and which imperial munificence distributed to the great churches, should bear the stamp of Rome. Thus the art of the Carolingian and, after them, the Ottonian treasures was deliberately archaistic—in other words, classical. In virtue of its techniques, its feeling for plastic values and all it owed to Mediterranean humanism, it was diametrically opposed to the Romanesque aesthetic. In the time of Suger this artistic tradition was still alive; it persisted in Saxony, cradle of the Ottonian line, and, more vigorously, in cities of the Rhine and Meuse regions and in Lotharingia, most Carolingian of the provinces of Europe. This was the home of the bronze-workers, of the only true statuary art of the age and of the most expert enamellers.

When the abbot of Saint-Denis decided to assemble a treasure worthy of his abbey and the majesty of the kings of France, who were now beginning to feel qualified to take over the heritage of Charlemagne and, in their turn, to lead western Christendom on the pathway of salvation, he called in Lorrainese goldsmiths. The works of art produced by them were costly and extremely fragile. The function of the treasure was not merely ornamental; it also constituted a reserve of wealth which could be drawn on in emergencies. Periodically, when it was proposed to "modernize" the artefacts owned by the royal abbey, the old ones were broken up. This is why so few of the objects commissioned by Suger have survived: only some sacred vessels in sard or crystal, remakes of vessels of antique or Arab provenance. Nothing remains of the Great Cross of Gold which he set up in 1140 above the tomb of St Denis; it is represented, however, on a painted panel of the fifteenth century, and a small-scale replica of its foot is preserved at Saint-Omer. This last was made some thirty years later by another Mosan artist, Godfrey of Claire (or Huy). Its decoration tells us something of Suger's theological program, his wish to demonstrate the concordances between the Old and New Testaments by means of juxtaposed scenes. The base is supported by gilt-bronze statuettes of the four Evangelists, whose writings are fundamental to the Christian faith, and on the shaft are four enamel plaques representing Old Testament prefigurations of the life of Jesus: Moses and the brazen serpent, Isaac carrying the wood for the burnt-offering, Aaron tracing on the brows of the Chosen the Tau symbol (the pre-Christian cross), Joshua bringing back the bunch of grapes from the Promised Land. On the capital figure the four elements of the Cosmos.

Starting from Saint-Denis, this typological symbolism spread throughout the Christian West, then engaged in a bitter struggle with the Cathar heresy; these images testified to the truth of the Redemption. The enamel plates on a portable altar preserved in the treasure of the Abbey of Stavelot, in Lorraine, also bore effigies of Isaac, the brazen serpent, Melchizedek and Abel, and the intricate iconography of the Klosterneuburg ambo, decorated about 1180 by Nicholas of Verdun, another craftsman from the Mosan region, is likewise based on the doctrine of concordances.

GODFREY OF CLAIRE (OR OF HUY). FOOT OF A CROSS FROM THE ABBEY OF SAINT-BERTIN, SECOND HALF OF THE 12TH CENTURY.
MUSÉE-HÔTEL SANDELIN, SAINT-OMER.

RELIQUARY SHRINE OF ST HERIBERT, ARCHBISHOP OF COLOGNE (DIED 1021), ABOUT 1160-1170.
CHURCH OF ST HERIBERT, COLOGNE-DEUTZ.

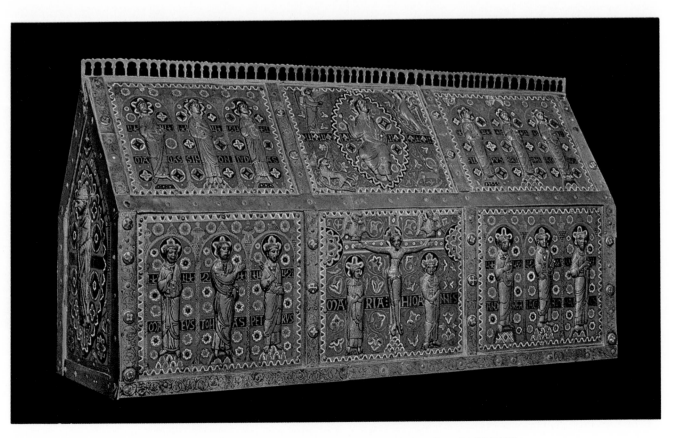

RELIQUARY SHRINE OF ST CALMIN, LATE 12TH OR EARLY 13TH CENTURY.
CHURCH OF SAINT-PIERRE, MOZAC, NEAR RIOM (PUY-DE-DÔME).

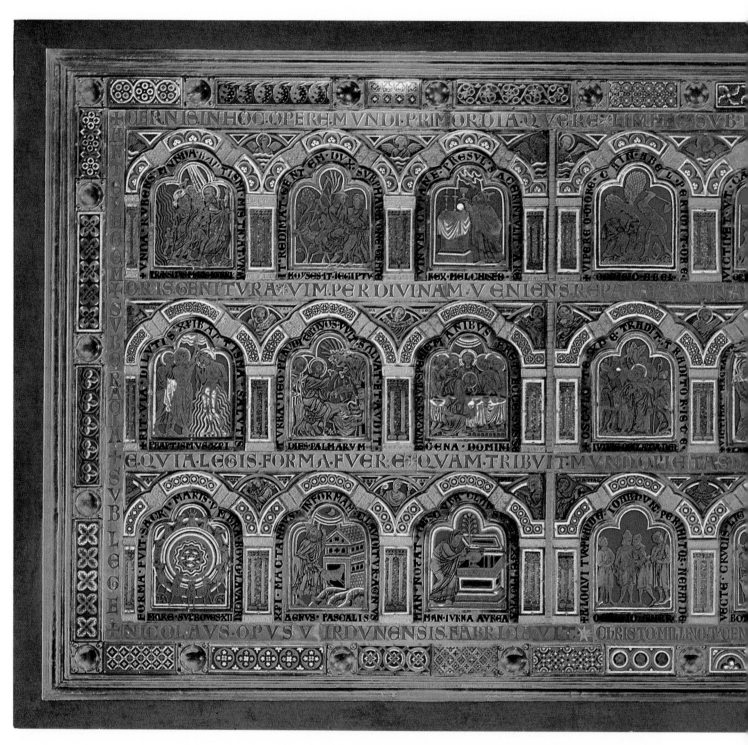

NICHOLAS OF VERDUN (ABOUT 1130-ABOUT 1205). KLOSTERNEUBURG ALTAR

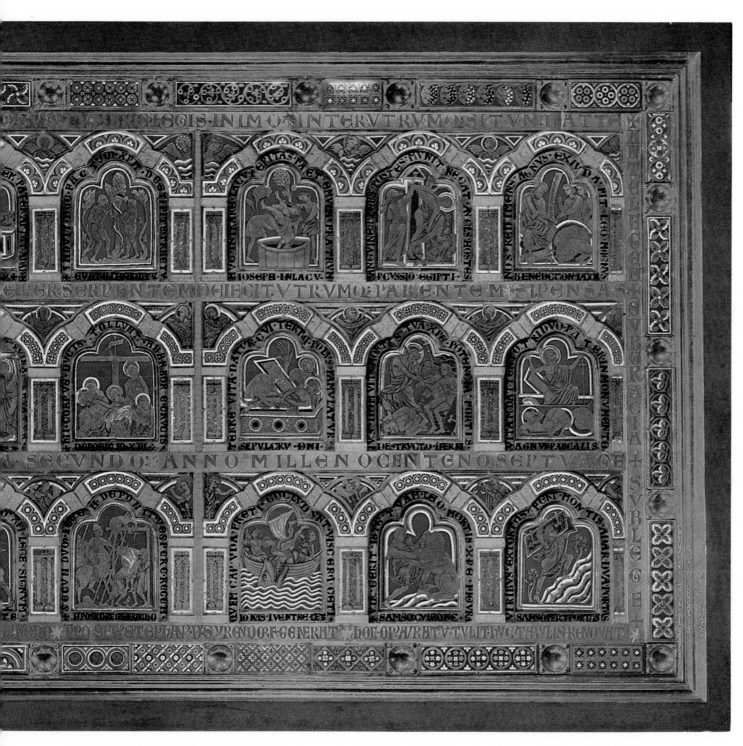

ABOUT 1180. ABBEY MUSEUM, KLOSTERNEUBURG, NEAR VIENNA.

God is Light and the interior of His church prefigures the heavenly Jerusalem whose walls, the Book of Revelation tells us, are made of precious stones. The function of the stained-glass window is to admit the light of day and in so doing to transmute it, embellish it, invest it with the hues of the various gems—rubies, topazes, emeralds, lapis lazuli—which according to the ancients were endowed with magical virtues corresponding to specific properties of the soul. The art of the stained-glass window is bound up with that of the reliquaries and chalices, and of the altar incorporated in the sacred edifice. Playing on these holy objects, the light streaming through it bathes the interior in an iridescent sheen, a splendor heralding the glories of the after-life and creating an atmosphere of ecstatic awe. But, like the enamels on pulpits, crosses and reliquaries, the window also had a didactic purpose, that of a proclamation of the Christian verities. Its imagery set the thoughts of the congregation on the path of holy meditation leading to true belief.

Suger, then, transposed the message of edification, which the officiating priests could "read" at close quarters on the Great Cross of the high altar, on to the windows of the choir so as to make it visible to the entire congregation. As in Ottonian Gospel books and Mosan enamels, this imagery formed a well-ordered sequence, combining all the themes that were henceforth basic to Catholic propaganda and affirmed the validity of the Incarnation as against the doctrines of the heretics. Soon these same themes were transferred from the windows to the illustrated pages of religious books and the sculpture in church portals. The Cross held the central place. The windows of Saint-Denis were a visual equivalent of the homiletics of the monastic schools. They interpreted the Scriptures, revealed their hidden meanings and proved that the Old Testament contained intimations, antetypes, of the New. And to demonstrate the unity of God in Three Persons, Suger showed the Trinity as a group surrounded by the four Evangelist symbols: God the Father upholding Christ crucified, linked to His image by the Dove, the Holy Spirit.

Little by little the symbolism of the Old Testament concordances gave place to themes centering on the Passion; characters from Genesis and Exodus were replaced by images of the participants in the tragedy of Calvary. On the Crucifixion window in the cathedral of Poitiers, Jesus is shown (following a tradition transmitted by the ninth-century ivory carvers) still alive on the cross, with the Virgin, St John, the lance bearer and the man holding the sponge beside Him.

SCENES OF THE LIFE OF MOSES AND ALLEGORY OF THE CHURCH, ABOUT 1140-1144.
STAINED-GLASS WINDOWS IN THE CHAPEL OF SAINT-PÉRÉGRIN, CHURCH OF SAINT-DENIS.

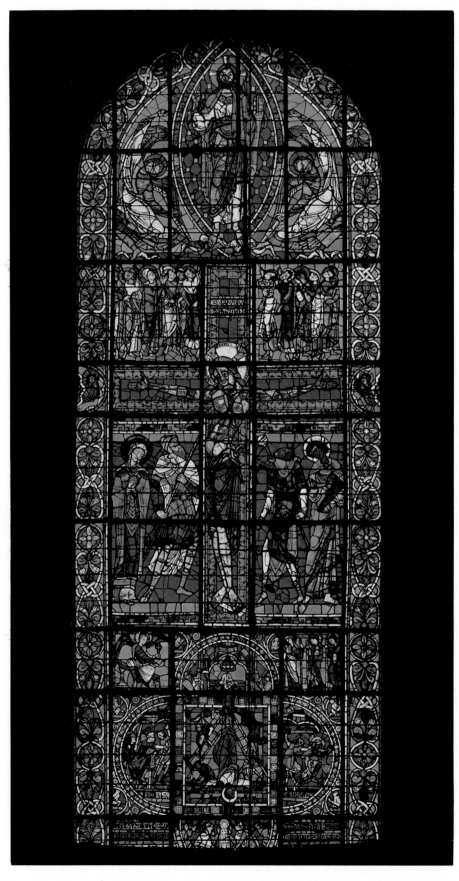

THE CRUCIFIXION, ABOUT 1165. DETAIL OF A STAINED-GLASS WINDOW, CATHEDRAL OF SAINT-PIERRE, POITIERS.

FLOREFFE BIBLE: THE CRUCIFIXION, ABOUT 1170. FOLIO 187, ADD. MS 17738, BRITISH MUSEUM, LONDON.

THE TREE OF JESSE

The high nobility to begin with, then the knights, had set much store on lineal descent. This deep respect for ancestry, basic to the fame and fortune of the aristocratic families and to the prestige of every feudal lord, was undoubtedly the factor which, more than any other, maintained the cohesion of the social order during this period. Every canon, every knight was conscious of his lineage, of being the scion of a noble House, and cherished the memory of his forbears. Hence came the notion of a family tree rooted in the ancestral soil and spreading out across the years in many branches. So when in the twelfth century the Church affirmed its faith in the humanity of Christ and vigorously denounced the heretics who declared it impossible that the divine essence should commingle with the carnal, it illustrated its demonstration with a genealogical symbol, the Tree of Jesse. According to Emile Mâle this image made its first appearance on one of the Saint-Denis windows, and the idea of a tree came from the layout of the text, dated 1100, of a manuscript from the abbey of Saint-Martial at Limoges. The "tree" contains images of all the persons mentioned in the Bible whose words foretold the coming of the Messiah, headed by Isaiah, who prophesied: "There shall come forth a rod out of the stem of Jesse, and a Branch shall grow out of his root" (Isaiah, xi. 1). It is clear that the prophet had a lineage in mind. In its simplified form this motif is composed of three figures, one above the other, rising from the loins of Jesse: King David, Mary, and her Son. Thus the notion of a celestial dynasty was grafted on to that of an earthly dynasty, and sublimated it. In the brilliantly illuminated choir the initial symbol figuring in the porch recurs, but with an added emphasis and greater luminosity. Begun on the threshold of the church with a cortège of stately figures of the Old Dispensation, prophets and the ancestors of Jesus, the sequence of images terminates with the Tree of Jesse.

Thirteenth-century liturgical books and all the objects in the treasure have the air of replicas of the cathedral. Typical is the Saint-Taurin reliquary shrine, decorated in 1240 and 1255. The commission for this, clearly a Parisian work, was given by St Louis and it bears the heraldic emblem of the King of France; fleurs-de-lys and Castilian castles adorn this reliquary, from whose upper part rise stylized ears of wheat. It is given the form of a church with a transept and belfry above the crossing. Like the new cathedrals, it projects skywards a fantastic tangle of pinnacles, finials and gables, the architecture of an imaginary city, symbolizing the heavenly Jerusalem.

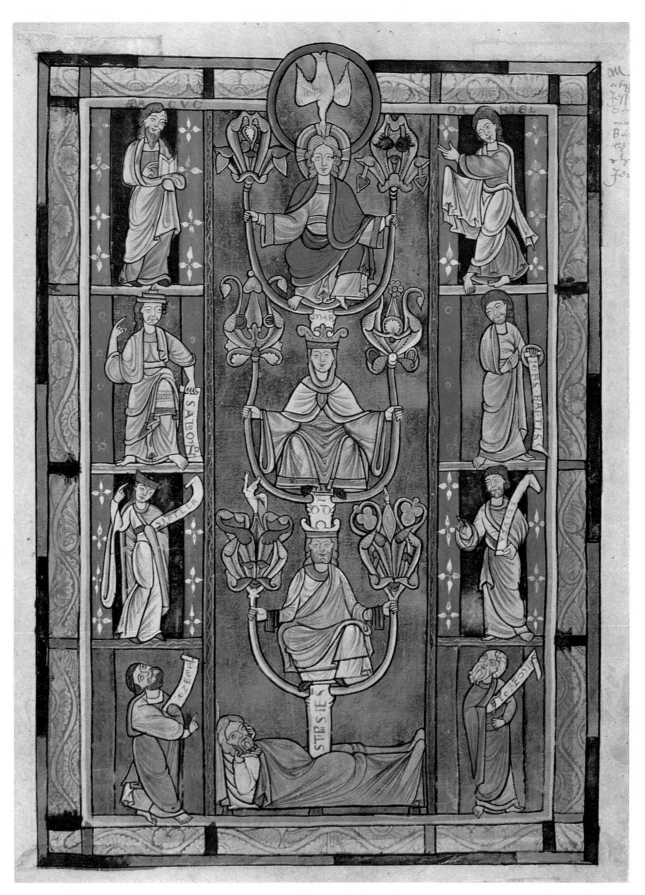

RABANUS MAURUS, "DE LAUDIBUS SANCTAE CRUCIS": THE TREE OF JESSE, SECOND HALF OF THE 12TH CENTURY.
FOLIO 11, MS 340, BIBLIOTHÈQUE MUNICIPALE, DOUAI.

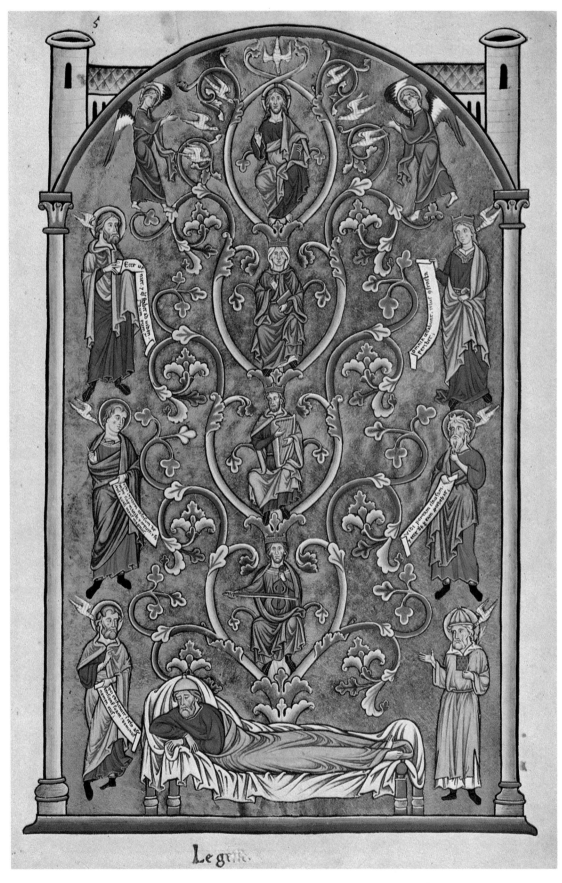

PSALTER OF QUEEN INGEBURGE: THE TREE OF JESSE, EARLY 13TH CENTURY. MUSÉE CONDÉ, CHANTILLY.

THE TREE OF JESSE, 12TH CENTURY. STAINED-GLASS WINDOW TO THE RIGHT OF THE ROYAL PORTAL, CHARTRES CATHEDRAL.

RELIQUARY SHRINE OF ST TAURIN, 1240-1255. CHURCH OF SAINT-TAURIN, ÉVREUX.

THE CITY CHURCH

A true son of St Benedict, Suger was an abbot and the abbey he built—if in a sense the most "urban" of its kind—was essentially a monastery church. But the men who carried on his work were bishops, prelates of the now renascent towns. From the stained-glass windows of Saint-Denis stemmed, in the mid-twelfth century, those of Chartres, Bourges and Angers, all of them cathedrals; from its column-statues those of Chartres, Le Mans and Bourges. The architectural innovations of Saint-Denis were followed up between 1155 and 1180 at Noyon, Laon, Senlis, Paris and Soissons, all in the lineage of the cathedrals of Neustria. A natural affiliation, since for Suger the power of the consecrated king rested less on the feudal hierarchy than on the Church, and he saw in the bishops, as in the time of the emperors Louis I the Pious and Charles the Bald, the true pillars of royalty. This shift of artistic activity from the abbey to the cathedral was a symptom of the vast changes that were taking place in the social structure and the rapid growth of urban life in northern Gaul.

Towns had been almost completely obliterated in the forests of the Carolingian age. Now that the land was being reclaimed for cultivation, they took a new lease of life. Being a "lord," whether of the Church or of a domain, meant living in luxury and a rank above that of the common people. Every owner of a large estate felt as in duty bound to wear rich garments, and to provide good wine and exotic fare at his banquets. Thanks to the new prosperity of agriculture, the feudal lords could gratify these tastes, and they also enriched the boatmen, known as "marchands de l'eau," who plied a thriving trade on the great rivers—Seine, Oise, Aisne and Marne—and had their headquarters in Paris. The vendors of wine, spices and colored textiles prospered, and by the end of the eleventh century Italian traders were making their appearance on the roads of France. Sixty years later, in Champagne, there developed the great fairs, soon to become the chief centers of international commerce. The merchants of those days were roving adventurers, perpetually on the move, but they had offices and warehouses in the towns, which they thus helped to repeople. In the far north of Gaul the Romans had founded few towns and these few had fallen to pieces irreparably in the dark age of barbarism. So now new towns sprang up at the most promising spots, usually near a castle or a monastery. In the heart of Neustria, however, the old Roman towns were more thickly populated and more active than ever. Merchants built houses at the foot of the walls and a whole new quarter developed along the river bank, at the points where barges were moored, beside the marketplace. As business intensified throughout the twelfth century the marketplace was steadily enlarged. Ramshackle huts with wooden or wattle walls housed negotiable goods of considerable value, no longer the visible produce of the land as in the old days, but now consisting of ingots, spices, bales of merchandise of various kinds, and large sums of money were made available for operations in foreign currency and loans. It was from these hoards, kept secret to evade the tax collector, that the bishop and his chapter of canons, lords of the city and its environs, drew the funds for rebuilding the local cathedral.

For the old cathedral seemed sadly out of date. No building had been done in this part of France during the tenth century, when the region was infested with pirates, Northmen who looted everything they could lay hands on. Nor was any done in the eleventh, the century when the countryside was being slowly reclaimed for cultivation. Now, however, money was pouring in; the canons were taking a hand in trade, selling the wheat and wine of their domains and trafficking in the tithes. They levied taxes on the ports and markets, which despite evasions were extremely fructuous. The townsfolk were their "men," that is to say their subjects, liable to a *taille* and a capitation tax.

The bourgeois was known to be well off and the Church authorities deliberately squeezed him, confiscating on occasion his casks of wine and bale goods. Thus a large part of its wealth was drained off from a section of the population that was steadily becoming larger and more affluent. Sometimes the victims retaliated and in an atmosphere of rioting and violence banded together in a town commune, a fighting force. In the course of these disturbances some of the canons and sometimes the bishop himself lost their lives, but sooner or later a settlement was arrived at. A charter was drawn up giving the townsfolk partial emancipation from their lords and there was a show of regulating taxation. Yet, appearances notwithstanding, the outcome was always in effect a stiffening of the claims of the cathedral chapter on the wealth of the community.

Money flowed in, perhaps even more abundantly, through another channel, that of voluntary alms. For the rich tradesfolk had uneasy consciences; they were told that "no merchant can find favor in the eyes of God," since he enriches himself at the expense of his fellow men. In twelfth-century France the practice of trade was still regarded as a sin. When he felt his end approaching the businessman, feeling qualms about his future lot, tried to free himself from his burden of sin by making a generous donation. This he could do all the more easily because his wealth was his alone and not, like the landed estates of the nobility, the common property of a family whose members saw to it that their patrimony was not dilapidated and sometimes even sought to recover from the Church the legacies of too generous ancestors. Formerly the rural nobility had been lavish givers—the prosperity of the monasteries was due to their largesse—but they were now becoming parsimonious. In the reigns of Louis VII and Philip Augustus a flood of pious donations poured in from the new-rich merchants, most of them no longer in the form of land but in cash, with the result that a large proportion of the money circulating in the shops and on the money-changers' tables found its way into the hands of the bishop and the chapter. Moreover any prelate who embarked on the building of a new cathedral could count on receiving a large sum from the king, always the most generous of donors. This was especially the case when the bishop was a relative, brother or cousin of the king, for then the latter could easily secure lucrative prebendal canonries for sons of vassals or members of the clergy serving in his chapel. Hence the remarkable fact that so many French cathedrals were created almost simultaneously.

Amply supplied with funds from all these sources, the bishop could give free rein to his ambitions, chief of which was the celebration of his power and personal prestige. For he not only ranked as a *grand seigneur* but also wished his name to live on the lips of men. A new cathedral seemed to him an exploit, a battle won. Reading Suger's description of his building activities at Saint-Denis, we feel he is consumed with vanity. This desire for personal renown accounts for the spirit of competition which within twenty-five years came to possess, one by one, all the bishops in the royal domain and later, at Reims, led the archbishop to have himself represented, surrounded by his suffragans, on the large windows of the cathedral, and to reconstruct the portal so that it should be even more sumptuous than the one recently built by his rival, the bishop of Amiens.

The bishop's church, as now rebuilt, signified also the alliance of Melchizedek and Saul, that is to say the effective union of episcopal power and royalty. No less than Saint-Denis, Reims was a royal monument. Here, too, there were engaged towers built into the façade and the same ambivalent column-statues, in which the townsfolk recognized the figures of Philip of France and Queen Agnes rather than those of Solomon and the Queen of Sheba. And, finally, the new cathedral vaunted the prosperity of the town and its inhabitants, of the many shops and workyards all of which had contributed to its erection and above which it towered majestically. It symbolized the pride of a middle class that had come into its own. With a profusion of spires, pinnacles and gables fretting the sky it conjured up visions of the ideal City of God, a sublimation of the earthbound city spread out at its foot. Whenever the communes chose their seals their choice fell on a design showing the profile of the cathedral; there could be no better emblem of their power. Its towers kept watch and ward over their industries and trade, and its nave provided the only covered expanse in the center of a town which elsewhere was little more than a huddle of narrow alleys, drains and piggeries. The cathedral was not only a place of worship; it was here that the guilds assembled and it was the meeting place of the entire population on great occasions.

Moreover the status of being a "man" of the Church ensured certain privileges and exemptions from customs tariffs, of whose value the local merchants were fully conscious. This was one of the reasons why the merchant class regarded this splendid monument, on which they prided themselves and which they had adorned, as theirs. At Amiens the dealers in the dyes used for textiles felt that their renown was enhanced, if indirectly, by the beauties of the cathedral; at Chartres each of the guilds insisted on having its own stained-glass window. Huge sums of money were spent on these edifices which, without exhausting the wealth of the community, dedicated it to God's service, justified the opulence of the city and increased its fame. But it was not the wine merchants or drapers who directed building operations; that was left to experts, men of erudition.

In the twelfth century the only schools that still existed in Neustria, the western kingdom of the Franks, later called Normandy, were the cathedrals. During the dark Carolingian age the kings of the Franks had actively promoted a system of education modeled on Greek and Roman disciplines and founded large libraries and scriptoria. But, as was to be expected in a region whose population was entirely agricultural, where only students of theology and prelates had books at their disposal and where the abbeys were the keystone of the ecclesiastical edifice, these instruments of knowledge were available only in the monasteries. For several centuries education had been almost a monopoly of the monks; they trained novices, and the children of the nobility were their pupils. The king sent his sons to study at Saint-Denis. Even in the eleventh century, after the troubles due to the decline of the imperial power, when the church had lapsed into the comparative rusticity of the age of chivalry, the monastic schools still maintained their prestige as centers of learning in northern Gaul. After 1100, however, their influence rapidly waned, they tended to keep to themselves, to restrict their educative functions to the monastic communities and no longer to diffuse knowledge. For the new impulse to asceticism cut off still more the cloister from the world. The Benedictine's duty was to pray, to seek God in isolation, and teaching was henceforth the specific task of the priesthood. Of the bishop to begin with; but he was too much of a *grand seigneur* to teach in person; too busy sitting in the royal court, passing judgments or, on occasion, clad in armor, leading military expeditions. Most of the time he delegated his administrative duties to the priests attached to his church, to the canons and in particular to the one who was put in charge of the school. The precincts of the cathedral (always called the cloister, though not enclosed by walls) were usually crowded with pupils. This tendency to shift the educational activities of the monastery towards the cathedral was paralleled by a similar movement which led to the formation of centers of creative art in many of the larger towns. Both were due to the changes that were coming over the social structure as a result of improved communications, intensified commercial activity and facilities for traveling —all of which speeded up the innovations taking place in the field of ecclesiastical art.

Thus the teaching in the cathedral schools proceeded on new lines, and became less withdrawn, more accessible to the contemporary world-view. The abbeys had shunned the outside world, secluded themselves from it by walls that the monks were not allowed to cross—they were already half way to their true home in heaven. In the monastery education was seldom given in groups, more usually in pairs: every novice was assigned to the tutelage of a senior monk who supervised his course of reading, initiated him, and led him step by step along the path of meditation. But the cathedral school consisted of classes; groups of disciples sat at the feet of a master who read out to them a set book and commented on it. And these students were not isolated from the world but free to roam the streets of the town and to share in its life. Needless to say all or almost all were destined to a career in the Church; they were "clerks," wore the tonsure and were subject to the bishop's jurisdiction. Learning was of the nature of a religious rite. But the training they were given prepared them for an active life; it was both secular and evangelical, for their mission was to preach, to familiarize the populace at large with the Word of God.

The new world that the march of progress was calling into being after an age of darkness and relative barbarism had need of men capable of thinking clearly and expressing themselves. These youngsters who, turning from the profession of arms and a life at the courts of chivalry, had elected for the service of God knew well that only if they developed their minds would they qualify for the best posts in the Church. So they flocked to the cathedral school, where the number of students was growing. But these numbers fluctuated, increasing or diminishing according to the capacities of the teachers. The word went round that this or that cathedral chapter had a particularly well-stocked library, that the man in charge was more learned, more competent than the average and that students trained by him would have a better chance of advancement. Soon, certain schools eclipsed the others and intellectual activities tended to center in some major institution where the pupils had the choice of several professors, could change from one to the other, and where the disciplines were planned not to overlap. At the close of the eleventh century Chartres and Laon were the cathedral schools which attracted most pupils. That by the time when Suger's work on Saint-Denis was completed Paris was by way of supplanting them was largely due to the prestige of Abelard, most brilliant teacher of the age. In 1150 the royal city was crowded with students who came not only from the countryside of the Ile-de-France but also from Normandy, Picardy, the Germanic lands and, above all, England, to profit by his teaching. This took place in the cloister of Notre-Dame, but there now was also another center on the left bank of the Seine, on the Montagne Sainte-Geneviève. Meanwhile other, more independent teachers the boldness of whose ideas won them a following among the younger men rented booths on the Petit Pont (Rue du Fouarre). In 1180 an Englishman who had studied in Paris founded a school for poor students. South of the Seine a new student quarter, facing the Ile de la Cité (residence of the royal household) and the Pont au Change (the business center), was in process of formation. The great city, which was to be the vital center of the art of France, was now assuming its triple role—royal, commercial, educational—and in the narrow streets of the student quarter a new spirit was coming to birth.

Within the monasteries, and still at Saint-Denis, studying meant a discipline based on contemplation, solitary musings on the scriptures, a graduated progress towards enlightenment by way of symbols and analogies—little different from prayer and choral singing. But at Chartres, Laon and Paris the same dynamism that animated the businessmen in their commercial enterprises urged the young students to intellectual adventures. They did not only read and meditate, they discussed; masters and students confronted each other in wordy jousts, in which the former were not always the victors. Often indeed the classes at the cathedral school had all the air of tournaments, contests of verbal prowess which, like the knightly lists, trained the young men to hold their own in combat. In his youth Abelard had made his name in these open contests and, like a hero of chivalry, had achieved not only fame but triumphs in the lists of love.

Though it covered a wider field, the teaching in the cathedral schools kept to the old curriculum of the "liberal arts" which the scholars of the court of Charlemagne had, long before, unearthed in certain didactic treatises, a legacy of Late Antiquity. The only novelty was that, after the first third of the twelfth century, the elements of the medieval *Trivium* came more and more to be treated as preparatory to what was regarded as the chief function of the clerk: detailed commentation of the Holy Scriptures with a view to clarifying and demonstrating the Christian verities. Students were still required to take a course of rhetoric and grammar. For the commentator of the Bible dealt with words, whose meaning and construction he had clearly to understand, and these were Latin words. With this in mind the masters read to the junior classes the great classical texts—Cicero, Virgil, Ovid—and their beauty was not lost on the more perceptive students. Abelard and many others, even St Bernard himself, retained their early enthusiasm for the Latin poets throughout their lives. This teaching gave the pupils a bias towards humanism and the education provided in the schools of the larger towns did much to instill a taste for the values of Antiquity and a feeling for the human into the minds of those who planned the decorations of the new cathedrals. Now that their eyes were opened, they lost interest in Romanesque forms and tended to prefer Carolingian ivories, the art of the first renaissance, the plastic values of Mosan enamels. It is in the schools of Chartres and Orléans, where more attention than elsewhere was directed to the study of the humanities, that we can trace the source of the renascent current that carried to the portal of Reims Cathedral the classicizing figures of the Visitation.

But this applies only to a preliminary phase. At Laon, and above all in Paris, dialectic soon came to be regarded as the major element of the *Trivium*. And this, the art of reasoning, the exercise of *ratio*, now ranked highest among the faculties of the educated man. Reason, Berengar of Tours (died 1088) had declared, was "the honor of man" and his "specific light," that reflection of the celestial light which is man's prerogative. To the professors and their disciples, the "intellectuals" of the age, intelligence seemed the most effective weapon, the only one capable of defeating error and enabling comprehension of the mystery of the divine. Since all our ideas stem from the mind of the Creator and since they are often set forth imperfectly, in veiled, obscure, sometimes even contradictory terms in the Scriptures, it is the task of logical reasoning to dispel these shadows and resolve these contradictions. The first thing is to examine the *word* and find out its inner meaning, but this must be done by the strict dialectic method and not by a surrender, as in the monasteries, to the vagaries of meditation. Each problem must be tackled with an open mind. "By doubting we are led to inquire: by inquiry we perceive the truth," Abelard says in *Sic et Non*, in which he assembled contradictory statements of the Fathers, with a view to reconciling them. He begins by setting forth the texts separately, brings his mind to bear on them, interprets them from different angles, discusses their possible meanings, weighs these up, then formulates conclusions, "sentences." Many contemporaries regarded this rationalistic approach as presumptuous, perilous, even diabolical. Abelard justified it on practical grounds. "My students," he said, "asked for human and philosophical reasons, intelligible explanations, rather than categorical assertions. They said it was useless to talk if one did not make one's statements meaningful; no one can believe what he has not begun by understanding."

That during the period this dialectical procedure made such rapid strides was largely due to the progressive assimilation of a methodology which western thinkers were discovering in cultural areas lying outside the domain of Latin Christendom and better provided with the instruments of logical exegesis. It now was possible to draw on the philosophic wealth of the Moslem world and through its intermediacy on that of ancient Greece. After vanquishing Islam the Christians pillaged the intellectual hoard of their defeated foe. No sooner was Toledo reconquered than teams of Latin and Jewish scribes started translating Arab texts and versions of Greek writers. While the armies which were gradually driving back the Infidels from the continent were mainly composed of French knights, the intellectual exploitation of their triumphs in the field was the work of the priests of France. The chief gainers by the translations made in Spain were the schools of Neustria, primarily Chartres and to a less extent Paris. Their libraries were provided with the new books, notably the logical treatises of Aristotle. These furnished the masters with a compendium of dialectics of which the western monks had hitherto gleaned only a partial, vague idea by way of the works of Boethius. This is why such a man as John of Salisbury, who had studied in Paris in the years 1136-1148, spoke of Aristotle as "*The* Philosopher" and of dialectics as "queen of the *Trivium*." All intellectual advancement, he said, rested on dialectics, which by the exercise of *ratio* co-ordinates the experience of our senses, then by the exercise of *intellectus* relates all things to their divine Cause and apprehends the scheme of Creation, leading the thinker, step by step, to perfect knowledge, *sapientia*. In Paris Peter Lombard in his *Book of Sentences* developed the first logical analysis of the Biblical text, while Peter of Poitiers boldly asserted that "though surely certitude exists, it is meet for us to doubt the articles of faith, to search and to discuss."

From this doubt, these searchings and discussions, the new theology drew its strength—less emotional but more vigorous and more precisely ordered than its predecessor. Abelard had incurred the wrath of the monks of Saint-Denis by being first to put forward the view that the titular saint of the abbey was not the same person as Dionysius the Areopagite, and he had the courage to propound another *Theologia*, also based on illumination. "The light of the material sun is not the result of our own efforts to apprehend it, but flows over us *per se* so that we may enjoy it. Likewise we come near to God in so far as He himself approaches us, bestowing on us His light and the warmth of His love." For the professors, then, God was Light, and the cathedrals that now were built were even more luminous than Saint-Denis. But they also became more "evangelical," in that the teaching of the schools tended more and more to relate the Old Testament to the New, to lay more emphasis on the Incarnation and to rely more strongly on the first chapter of the Gospel of St John and all the passages describing the Word of God as the *vera lux* by which all things were created, that light of life which illuminates every man when he comes into the world. By the masters of the urban schools, more mindful of strict logic and wishing more clearly to define what their words meant, God was not so often viewed as that nucleus of dazzling light whose supreme effulgence still blinded the eyes of the monastic theologians; they saw Him, rather, in man's image. Like them, Christ was a Doctor who disseminated the light of the understanding; like them, carried a book and, like them was a teacher—their brother.

Their teaching aimed at clarity. It freed man from the thrall of formalism, emphasized the will behind his acts. Did not Abelard, writing to Heloise, affirm that "crime consists in the intention not in the evil deed"? It practised the analytical method, progressively resolving a complex datum into its parts, and asserted that "only the individual exists in its own right." It represented reality as an aggregate whose unity (like that of the new cathedral) was a sum of discrete elements. It directed attention to Nature; for as Abelard pointed out "there are forces operating in seeds and plants, in the essences of trees and stones, which can stimulate or tranquillize your souls." It described—and the sculpture in the cathedrals followed suit—the created world as it presents itself to the eye. Thierry of Chartres made an interpretation of the Book of Genesis, first of its kind to be based not on symbols but on new discoveries in the field of physics. He reduced God's work to the interaction of the basic elements of the cosmos and its concentric spheres. Fire, the lightest element, tended to escape towards the outmost verge of Space; water, in evaporating, gave birth to the stars; heat to life and all existing living beings. Ceasing to be a bewildering complex of signs, the universe became a logical configuration which it was the cathedral's mission to body forth by assigning all visible creatures to their proper places. It was the duty of the geometrician, using the deductive science of mathematics, to translate men's visions of the heavenly Jerusalem, evoked in the previous age by the ethereal, many-colored radiance of stained glass windows, into the concrete reality of stone.

For mathematics (another acquisition from the culture of conquered Islam) now bulked large in the training of professors and reinforced the discipline of logic. In Spain and southern Italy the members of the clergy who accompanied the leaders of the Christian reconquest discovered little by little in Arab treatises not only the philosophy of ancient Greece but her science too. Translations of Euclid and Ptolemy, also of manuals of algebra, were made for use in the schools of Chartres. Geometry and arithmetic were given a leading place in the new revised *Trivium* and in his *Didascalion* the Parisian *scholasticus* Hugh of Saint-Victor ranked the mechanical beside the liberal arts. At Saint-Denis the layout of a building had been for the first time "determined with the help of instruments of geometry and arithmetic" and it seems clear that for the plan of the crypt, where allowance had to be made for ninth-century substructures, recourse was had to diagrams and compasses. Thanks to these methods the new architecture had nothing of the makeshift character of so much Romanesque; logical planning overcame the handicaps of the material employed and made it possible to construct less narrow, less ponderous, more translucent edifices. The new "science of numbers" and the services of competent mathematicians played a large part in these architectural innovations and to them was due the invention in 1180 (in Paris) of the flying buttress which enabled the builders of Notre-Dame to increase the height of the nave. In recognition of their debt to the cathedral schools, French architects and artists often inserted figurations of the seven liberal arts in the basements of their churches. At the end of the twelfth century the art of France was in the hands of logicians; it was soon to become an art of engineers.

Very few pieces of the Saint-Denis treasure have survived, and next to nothing of the sculpture. Chartres, however, to which Suger's team of artists migrated about 1150 is fortunately intact. There, in the Royal Portal, the new art of France can be seen at its best. This art reflects the far-reaching changes which came over the climate of opinion in ecclesiastical circles at the turn of the century. At the schools of Chartres, Laon and Paris the new generation of churchmen had imbibed the teaching of the boldest spirits of the West and gradually learnt to turn away from the abstractions which had meant everything to their predecessors. The writings of Cicero, Ovid and Seneca told them that man is an individual who loves, suffers, pits himself against the coercive power of destiny. They took to analysing human emotions, the description of which was coming into vogue at the time when the Chartres workyard started. For the entertainment of the knights and high-born ladies, poets and troubadours were now composing elegant variations on antique themes, such as the adventures of Aeneas and the Trojan war. But, most important of all, an enlightened study of the Bible was providing them with a new image of God.

For these clerics, as for the artists who gave form to their ideas, the beautiful was that which most resembles God. Dazzled by the transcendent splendor of the God of Moses, Isaac and Jacob—the face whose blinding glory none can gaze on and which, to the human eye, has no apparent features—the monks of the year 1100 had made shift with symbolical equivalents. Their prayers were music and when they transposed them into figures, these did not represent any visual actuality, but intellectual concepts. But the God of the new bishops, canons and professors in the Ile-de-France was the Son of Man. For them he had assumed a human form, the face and body of a man. And so, for the rendering of the divine perfection, the artist no longer needed to take refuge in signs; he had but to open his eyes.

At Chartres, then at Le Mans, at Saint-Loup-de-Naud and Bourges, the statues of the Old Testament kings and the apostles were linked up with the walls and given the proportions of the columns from which they derived. There was no apparent life, no hint of movement, in the stiff, narrow, cylindrical bodies, strictly clad in robes with parallel flutings. Yet their faces were alive and little by little lost the formal symmetry appropriate to denizens of an abstract world. In 1185 when representing angels escorting heavenwards the sleeping Virgin, the Senlis sculptor no longer followed the pattern of the Gregorian antiphonals; he watched the flight of birds.

FAÇADE OF CHARTRES CATHEDRAL. MID-12TH CENTURY.

ROYAL PORTAL (WEST PORTAL) OF CHARTRES CATHEDRAL. 1145-1150.

KING SOLOMON, THE QUEEN OF SHEBA AND KING DAVID, 12TH CENTURY. STATUES IN THE SOUTH PORTAL OF BOURGES CATHEDRAL.

KINGS AND QUEENS OF JUDAH, 1145-1150. STATUES IN THE ROYAL PORTAL OF CHARTRES CATHEDRAL.

A KING OF JUDAH, 1145-1150. DETAIL OF A STATUE IN THE ROYAL PORTAL OF CHARTRES CATHEDRAL.

A KING OF JUDAH, 1145-1150. DETAIL OF A STATUE IN THE ROYAL PORTAL OF CHARTRES CATHEDRAL.

NAVE OF LAON CATHEDRAL. SECOND HALF OF THE 12TH CENTURY.

1

THE SPACE OF THE CATHEDRAL

The façades of the new churches proclaimed the sovereign might of God, the Lord. Garrisoned by the celestial hosts, the House of God was an impregnable stronghold. The powers of evil, the malignant influences it held at bay, could not prevail against it. This is why its form recalls a castle, or one of the stone keeps the barons built at the end of the eleventh century in the regions of the Loire and the Seine. Foursquare, massive, solidly constructed, the front of the cathedral held a commanding position. Like the crusades, it evidenced the military background of feudal society and reminded its members of their duties as soldiers of Christ. This is why a cohort of the Kings of Judah, who transmitted to Jesus, their offspring, the legacy of worldwide sovereignty, welcomed the Christian congregation on the threshold of a citadel.

In Neustria the structural elements of the building, symbolizing the grandeur of the Church, derived from a very old tradition. In planning the forepart of his basilica, Suger drew inspiration from the gatetowers of the Ile-de-France and, still more, from the tall façades of the Norman abbeys whose governors had served William the Conqueror. As early as 1080, when Normandy teemed with mail-clad warriors eager for adventure, it was usual to flank with towers the entrances of the sacred edifices patronized by the dukes, who drew from them the priests needed to reform the English church and keep it under control. These towers lay at the origin of the lofty walls which the Norman bishops built in conquered England, at Ely and Wells, at the forefront of their cathedrals.

When Suger included two towers like those of the Caen monasteries in the western block of Saint-Denis, he was introducing into the church that vehement upward drive which was to prevail until the close of the Middle Ages. Nevertheless the structure of the fore-church (devised by him), the storey of the high chapel and the rose window illuminating it, brought back the elevation to the horizontal. This interplay of the two dimensions, one stressed by buttresses and pilasters, the other by galleries and friezes, was to be a prime concern of the builders of the façades of Gothic cathedrals. But these façades never lost their original aspect, expressive of strength and victory. This victory of the Faith and the Word made flesh was bound to be of a military order in a community dominated by warriors, whose bishops, ever eager for a chance of leading their troops to battle, were escorted by helmeted vassals and whose ideal hero was the "Knight of Christ." In that age of a belligerent Christianity, the Kingdom of God was envisaged as a supernal stronghold.

Saint-Denis, prototype of the Gothic church, was an abbey church, built to be the scene of monastic liturgies; it adjoined the cloister and was connected with it by the transept. It was the private oratory of a closed community and if at times the public were admitted, they always seemed intruders. The cathedral, however, was the city church; it belonged to the clergy and the people, the bishop being their chosen representative, their "pastor." *Clerus et populus;* the cathedral, an open church, was equally at the disposal of the two orders of the Christian community. Actually, however, at the end of the eleventh century the Gregorian reform had emphasized the gap between the clergy and the congregation and the higher status of the former. Thus of the space within the cathedral walls the better part was reserved to the prelates and the building as a whole so arranged as to answer to the requirements of their sacred function. In practice this did not differ fundamentally from that of the monks; the chief

duty of the cathedral clergy was, like theirs, to chant the praise of God together at all hours of the day. Like that of the monastery church, the floor space of the cathedral was organized around the choir and provided passages for the free movement of ceremonial processions. The congregation occupied the back of the edifice near the entrance, or else (as in the basilicas of the pilgrimage monasteries) was relegated to galleries on the sides, overlooking the central nave. For the ordinary worshipper was, so far, only a spectator and though he attended the service did not take any active part in it.

Nevertheless the space within the cathedral differed in several ways from that of the basilicas attached to monasteries, and this for two reasons. One was that the clergy were far from being as segregated from the populace as were the monks. For in none of the lands specifically French had the cathedral clergy been subjected to the strict corporate discipline imposed by canonic law on priests of the Carolingian period. True, the French canons were an organized body, but they enjoyed a certain liberty and had not to live together between four walls. What was still called the "cloister" in French cities was in fact an open tract of ground near the cathedral, where every member of the chapter had a house of his own. And since there was no collective life there was no transept. This transverse passage crossing the central nave at right angles had ceased to serve any practical purpose; though it survives in Notre-Dame of Paris it does not project beyond the body of the edifice. Thus the space of the cathedral was by way of becoming self-contained, sufficient to itself.

The new theology of the *verum lumen* called for this structural unification; since light was both the manifestation of God Himself and the bond of union between Him and the human soul, it was fitting that the kingdom of God, demarcated symbolically by the walls of the cathedral, should be entirely filled with light. Therefore there were no breaks in the lines of bays, alternations of pillars and columns were abandoned, galleries eliminated, since they impeded the enlargement of the windows. Total unity is achieved in the Sainte-Chapelle—but this is essentially a reliquary shrine. Yet Bourges cathedral with its five naves side by side has no less unity.

THE SPACE OF THE CATHEDRAL

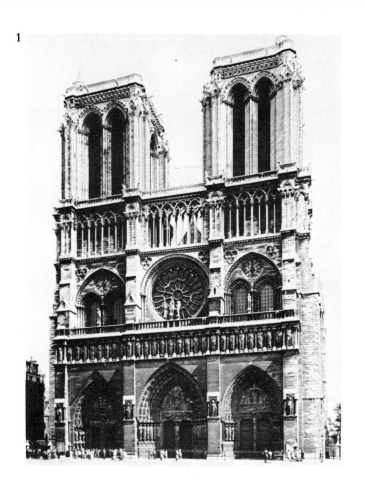

1

3

2

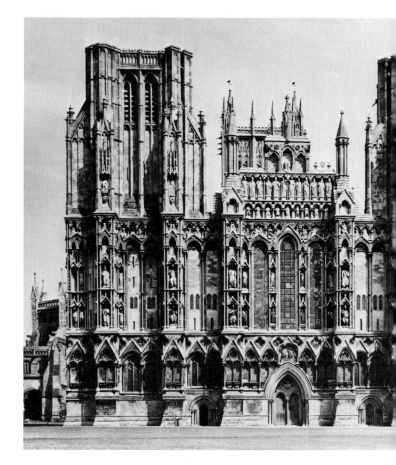

4

5

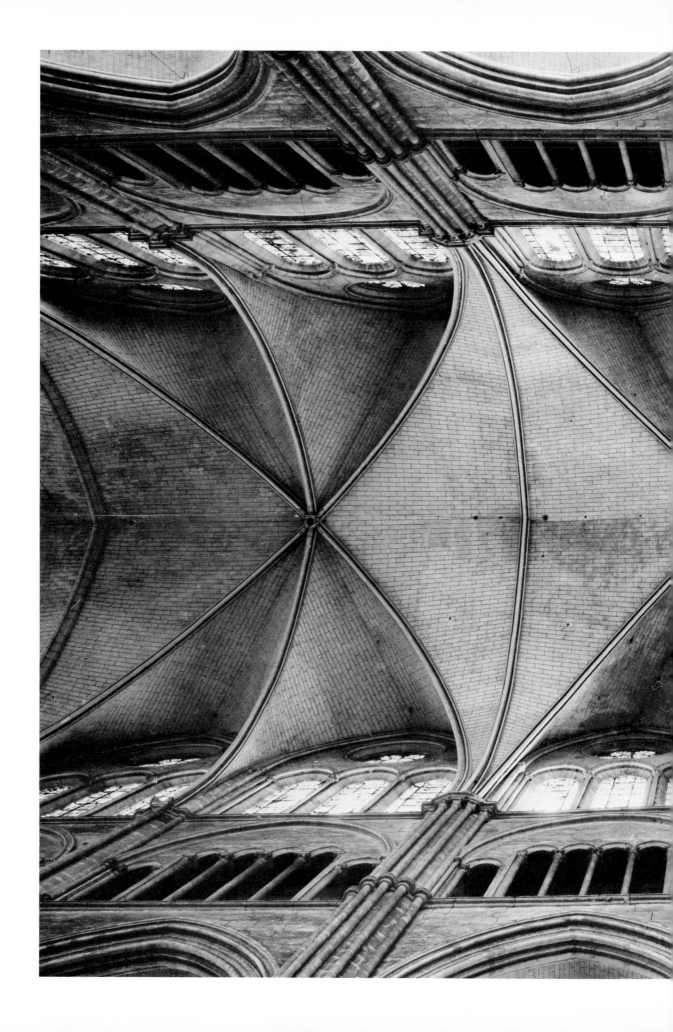

6

THE CISTERCIAN WAY

None the less the ideal of holiness prevailing at the time when the new cathedrals were being built was still essentially monastic in spirit. It was the age of Abelard and the flying buttresses of Notre-Dame that witnessed in the West the culmination of that spiritual trend which, after the triumph of the Christian faith, followed by the plight of Rome in the upheavals of the sixth century, had led to the belief that the surest way to salvation was a rejection of the world, its pomps and vanities. To the mind of the contemporaries of Philip Augustus, King of France (1180-1223), man's best means of escaping from the thrall of sin and saving his soul alive was plenary conversion, and this meant taking the Benedictine habit and retiring to the seclusion of a cloister. Not the open cloister of the canons and schoolmen, but that of the monks.

What was wanted, above all, was a new, reformed type of monasticism. The old interpretation of the Benedictine *regula*, the Rule of Cluny, which had been perfectly suited to the seigniorial structure of early feudalism, now seemed unacceptable. The Cluniac monks were accused of living like lords and yielding too readily to the spirit of the age. Exception was taken to their avoidance of manual labor, to that taste for comfort and display for which Suger seemed to have catered in his reorganization of Saint-Denis. The prosperity of the outside world, the new, unblushing zest for pleasure and easy living, led to a compensatory reaction: an idealization of poverty, withdrawal, self-supporting toil, total asceticism. Those who accepted this doctrine of austerity took for their exemplars the hermits who dwelt in forests and lived on herbs and roots. When, touched by divine grace, a knight decided to cut his earthly ties, to lay down his arms and to give up the pursuit of glory, he no longer entered a Cluniac abbey. That would not have meant a real break with the world of luxury and ostentation from which he wished to escape. He set to working as a charcoal burner. Thus round about the year 1100 several new religious orders were founded. Striking out in a new direction, the Carthusians elected for a monastic life of solitude and silence in the Oriental manner, in some desolate spot where the recluse "ate bread of unbolted meal and took so much water with his wine that it had hardly any flavor left." Other orders, however—and these were more in favor—practised a monachism less drastically opposed to that of Cluny and reconciling the Benedictine rule of communal life with asceticism. The year of the consecration of the choir of Saint-Denis, also the year when work began on the Royal Portal of Chartres, witnessed the triumph of another great monastic order, that of Citeaux. By 1145 there were over three hundred and fifty Cistercian houses in various parts of Western Europe, a Cistercian monk was elected pope (Eugenius III) and St Bernard's authority was everywhere paramount. We may dislike the personality of this violent, aggressive man who so brutally hounded down Abelard, who lashed the Roman Curia with invectives and strove persistently for temporal power. But it was he who launched crusades, counseled kings—and browbeat them—and went to Albi to preach against the heretic Cathars. When offered the archbishopric of Reims, he declined it and preferred to stay a monk. Under his dynamic leadership the White Monks won through to the conquest of the Church, and of the age.

This triumph, St Bernard's work, lasted after 1200; for many years Citeaux was still the alma mater of great bishops, a spearhead in the combat against heresy. Two hundred more abbeys were founded in the thirteenth century, Cistercians held many posts at the court of the French king and figured in the entourage of Blanche of Castile. Royaumont, the monastery that the sainted king preferred to all others, was a Cistercian foundation and he often stayed there, obeying the rule of the order, keeping silence and working with his hands, and he made the whole royal household do likewise.

"When a wall was being built around the Abbey of Royaumont, our sainted king often went there to attend Mass and other services or to inspect the work in hand. And since, observing the rule of Citeaux, the monks went after the hour of Tierce to carry stones and mortar for the wall that was a-building, the king too helped to bear the stretcher laden with stones, walking in front while a monk held it behind. Now and again our holy king had the stretcher carried by his brothers or by other knights of his household, and when sometimes his brothers were minded to talk, to shout or to play, the king admonished them: 'The monks are keeping silence, we should do as they do.' And once when his brothers had overloaded their stretcher and wished to rest on the path half way to the wall, he said to them: 'The monks do not rest, we too should not rest.' Thus our sainted king constrained his household to well-doing." Actually in the reign of St Louis the best days of Citeaux were over; pioneers of the great forward strides being made in agriculture, and profiting by them, the monasteries were becoming too rich, and the target of adverse criticism. Nevertheless the Cistercian mode of thought left a deep imprint on the age that saw the building of the first cathedrals.

Characteristic of the order was its antagonism to the cathedral schools. Cistercians heartily disapproved of the towns they had deliberately quitted, of the urban clergy whom they regarded as inferiors in the spiritual hierarchy, of the scholastic curriculum (futile in their eyes), and above all of Paris, the New Babylon, a hotbed of iniquity, especially pernicious to the young. In 1140 St Bernard himself had visited Paris with the sole aim of "converting" the students, that is to say inciting them to desist from their studies. The address he composed for their benefit, entitled *De Conversione ad Clericos*, counseled an escape from Babylon to the great open spaces, the desert, as the only means of salvation. The teachings of the masters, he said, "set up an uncalled-for screen betwixt the soul and Christ." Why, then, waste time on them? "You will find more in forests than in books; trees and rocks will teach you things no master can make known to you." In St Bernard's opinion any discussion of the scriptural message was a sin. Nothing, he said, is more injurious than dialectics, rational inquiry, vain attempts to make faith seem intelligible. He fiercely attacked the professors *en masse* at the council held

at Sens (1141) before which Abelard was arraigned, and again at the council at Reims where the "logic" of Gilbert de la Porée was similarly censured. Like Pierre de la Celle (the abbot of Saint-Remi of Reims whom Dante momentarily chose to be his guide in his spiritual journey) St Bernard held that "the true school, the one in which the pupil does not pay his teacher, in which there are no discussions" is the school of Christ. In point of fact Citeaux and the houses under Cistercian influence did not altogether prohibit meditation on the text of the Scriptures; they only gave it a new orientation, convinced as they were that the divine element in man consisted not in the reasoning faculty but in love; "understanding is nothing else than love."

In this way, combating the rationalistic approach of the "modern" philosophers, a new mode of religious thought was propagated by St Bernard and the Cistercians. Its fountainhead was the teaching of that pioneer of Latin mysticism, St Augustine, and this stream of thought attracted to itself the masters of certain cathedral schools less committed than the Parisian schools to the discipline of dialectics: notably the masters of the school of Chartres. As early as 1100 these latter had directed their pupils' attention to the few writings of Plato then available, fragments of the *Timaeus*. Suger's way of thinking owed much to them. Diffused by Chartres, these ideas, of Platonic inspiration and less appropriate to logical inquiry than to emotional effusion, found favor shortly after in another city school, in Paris itself. Not at Notre-Dame, but in the Abbey of Saint-Victor, a hermitage that, after being "converted," a learned canon had founded at the gates of the city. His disciples led an ascetic life and, as members of the clergy, continued to perform their religious duties as teachers. But what they inculcated was the Augustinian rule of contemplation. It would seem that the Victorines did not expressly condemn dialectics and philosophy; indeed Richard of Saint-Victor spoke in favor of the humanists and philosophers of Notre-Dame and the Montagne Sainte-Geneviève. The soul, he said, should exercise all its faculties, particularly the reasoning faculty; God is Reason and we can approach Him from this angle. But that is only one approach; nothing but love can elevate us to the highest sphere of knowledge, plenary inspiration. As for Hugh of Saint-Victor, like St Augustine—and like Suger—he declared that every perceptible image is a sign or "sacrament" of the things invisible, those that the soul will perceive when it has cast off its carnal garment. Following St Augustine, Hugh bade his disciples make the spiritual ascent towards this supreme vision, stage by stage. They must begin with *cogitatio*, an investigation of the visible, material world, for this is necessarily fundamental to all abstract thought; next, the inner man must rise higher, to the stage of *meditatio*, in which the soul looks inward at itself; then, finally, it attains the stage of *contemplatio*, intuitive knowledge of the truth. This doctrine was taken over by the Cistercians and it was in their houses, where the monks lived in total poverty, that the rules for this progress towards a contemplative enlightenment were most strictly observed. William of Saint-Thierry, who had dealings with the Carthusians in 1145, extolled the mediative power of love. As a humanist, he had enriched his mind with studies of such works as Cicero's *De Amicitia* and Ovid's *Ars Amandi*, the very works which were being read by the pupils in the cathedral schools of the Loire region. They were also studied by the troubadours in the princely courts, with a view to refining the theory of another, secular form of love, the so-called courtly love. Just as the knight was told to win his way into the heart of his ladylove by acts of martial prowess and by the sublimation of his grosser passions, so the disciples of William of Saint-Thierry were bidden to engage in a mystical ascent which, starting from the body, seat of animal life, moved ever higher to the soul, seat of Reason, and finally to the spirit, crown of all and seat of the sublimest ecstasy of love. By the light of love, true communion with God, "the soul passes from the world of shows and shadows into the full light of noonday, the supreme radiance of grace and truth."

The leading figure of the age, St Bernard, was a fervent champion of this doctrine. It was the pabulum with which he nourished day in, day out, his spiritual sons, the monks of Clairvaux, in one of the bays of the abbey. Profoundly impressed with the oneness of God, St Bernard fiercely resisted the dialecticians who called His unity in question: men like Abelard and Gilbert de la Porée who dissociated the Persons of the Trinity and whose rationalizing approach, incapable of elevating man to the mystical plane, tended to reduce God to the human status—to disaggregate Him. But how was the ineffable to be apprehended in its plenitude? An uncompromising ascetic, St Bernard believed that, for such an apprehension, complete poverty, that of the White Monks, was an indispensable preliminary. Only after vanquishing his body and climbing the "twelve steps of humility" could man hope to perceive himself as he truly is, an image of God. A faithful mirror, only falling short of the divine perfection by reason of the sin that tarnishes it. All that is needed is the uplift of love—and "the supreme cause of our love of God is God himself." The five Latin words composing this formula sum up the "back and forth movement" which in the *Hierarchies* of Dionysius governs the circulation of light. St Bernard keeps to the metaphor of light so frequently employed in the writings of the Pseudo-Areopagite, but he also uses others taken from the Song of Songs and these are of a nuptial order, for the union of the soul with God in states of ecstasy is of the nature of a wedlock, sealed by "the kiss of the spouse" (the soul). In this supreme moment there is an accord of wills, without confusion of substance, and the soul is "truly deified"; for what it then experiences is entirely divine. The soul is absorbed in this union as air flooded with sunlight is merged into the light, but it can achieve this union only if it is stripped of everything extraneous. "How can God be all in all if there remains in man something of man? True, the substance remains, but in another form, another glory, another power." On his upward way to the empyrean Dante placed his hand in St Bernard's.

Since St Bernard's ideas so closely approximated to the Dionysian theology, they should have led to an art resembling Suger's. But on one capital point the two men differed; St Bernard disapproved of outward show. The art of the Cistercian cloister and the church beside it was one of extreme austerity, eschewing any sort of adornment. Hence St Bernard's stern disapproval of Saint-Denis. "Not to mention the immense height and excessive breadth of your oratories, their sumptuous decorations and alluring paintings whose effect is to draw away the attention of the worshipper and hamper his meditation, and which recall after a fashion the rites of the Jews (for I am quite willing to grant that the purpose of all this is to glorify God), I shall in speaking to you, my fellow monks, use the same words that a pagan poet used, speaking to pagans like himself. 'What has gold to do,' he asked, 'in the temple?' And I, too, ask you, varying the poet's words and not his thought, what is the use for poor people like yourselves—assuming you are truly dedicated to poverty—of all the gold that glitters in your sanctuaries? The statue of a sainted man or woman is exposed to view and it is deemed the holier, the more it is bedecked with colors. Then people flock to kiss it and they are urged to donate alms; but it is to the beauty of the object rather than to its holiness that homage is being paid. Often, too, we see hung in churches what are rather wheels than crowns, spangled with gaudy beads, ringed round with lamps and inset with precious stones whose gleams are even brighter than those of the lamps. By way of candelabra there are veritable trees of brass wrought with wondrous skill, and the sheen of the gems is no less dazzling than that of the tapers they uphold. O vanity of vanities—but rather, I say, folly than vanity! The church is everywhere resplendent, but the poor are left destitute; its stones are clad in gold, but children go unclothed; lovers of beauty find in the church the wherewithal to gratify their taste, and the poor lack means to stave off their hunger."

St Bernard's conception of monasticism precluded ornamentation; there must be no more images in the House of God. Once his influence had taken effect in the Order, the White Monks ceased illustrating their books and the admirable school of painters that had flourished in earlier days came to a sudden end. The same fate befell monumental demonstrations of the Truth, the sculpture that had figured on the portals of the monasteries of Cluny. For the Cistercian abbey had no façade, not even a door; simple and devoid of ornament, it was isolated from the world. "Let those of us who are led by their concern for all that lies within to scorn and disregard what lies without, build for their worship edifices bearing the stamp of poverty, imitating the *sancta simplicitas* and wise restraint of their forefathers" (William of Saint-Thierry). By its very structure, the ordered sobriety of its parts and its symbolic layout, the abbey church, cornerstone and image of Christ, was meant to lead the soul towards the mystic heights. In its quiet precinct the light of day described the circles of the cosmic motion and traced the path of contemplation. No more was needed, for "it is not by a change of place," St Bernard said, "that we approach the Presence, but by successive enlightenments of a spiritual, not a physical order. Let the soul seek the light by following the light." Thus the sacred edifice was planned in terms of the discretion

native to the Rule of St Benedict. There is no straining upwards, no display, but a serene order conforming to the rhythm of the universe. Both in its mystique and in its handling of architectural volumes and their relations, Cîteaux carried on the Benedictine tradition and its churches were as sturdy and massive as the Romanesque churches of southern Gaul.

In two respects, however, its art resembled that of Saint-Denis and the first cathedrals. Primarily, in the emphasis given to light and its use of spacious bays adorned with stained-glass windows painted only in grisaille (with non-figurative motifs), giving free access to the light of day. For these openings in the walls of their churches the Cistercians kept to French structural methods, notably the usage of crossed pointed arches. The Order of Cîteaux, which originated in the east of the kingdom, began by establishing itself in Burgundy and Champagne, but affiliated abbeys soon sprang up in all parts of Latin Christendom and did much to diffuse the art of France, the *opus francigenum,* throughout the Christian world. It made its way even into the heart of the recalcitrant South; examples of it were to be found at Poblet in Catalonia and at Fossanova in central Italy. St Bernard also did much to promote the cult of the Virgin; he saw in her the "spouse" of the Song of Songs, the patroness of marriage, and under his aegis Cistercian art became a Marian art like that of the cathedrals.

Suger had included the Virgin in his schema of iconographic correspondences; had not the Mother of God participated in the Incarnation? But he assigned to her only a minor place in Saint-Denis. In the cathedrals of France, however, all of which were dedicated to Notre Dame, effigies of the divine motherhood figured in the center of the monumental decorations and on them was focused the devotion of the masses. Given the posture of the gilded "idol" of Romanesque Auvergne, these carved images did not as yet convey the emotion of love, but rather sovereignty and majesty. The Virgin Mother effaced the sins of womankind, put to flight evil spirits, impure dreams and sinful desires, and, in a sense, atoned for them. To her were directed the mystical yearnings of all these men who were striving for chastity, of the canons on whom attempts were now being made to enforce the rule of celibacy and, needless to say, of the monks of Cîteaux.

The Virgin made a majestic entrance, escorted by a company of sainted women, into the piety of the twelfth century. The Magdalen, sinner, hope of fallen women, triumphed at Vézelay and in Provence. And as it so happened, at the very time when Christendom was beginning to concern itself with feminine values, the exaltation of woman in the courts of chivalry in the Loire and Poitou regions was getting under way. There songs were being composed extolling the beauty of the great lord's wife, the singer's "ladylove," all the young nobles were trying to win her heart, and dalliance with the rites of "courtesy" was becoming one of the most exciting games in vogue at gatherings of the nobility. The cult of the Virgin and that of the ladylove had of course quite different origins, deep-seated but obscure, of which history tells us little. Yet they certainly had something in common. This much is clear: the note of passion struck for the first time in the West in Heloise's letters to Abelard, the Latin poems that Abbot Baudry of Bourgueil wrote for the Angevin princesses, the songs composed by Cercamont and Marcabru for the boudoirs of the ladies of Aquitaine and all the romances based on ancient themes, on the story of Aeneas and the Fall of Troy—the first tales whose episodes were not only of a military but of an amorous nature—link up with William of Saint-Thierry and the interpolations from Ovid in his *De Natura Amoris*. The same humanist sources, the same vocabulary, the same sequences of "ordeals," the same desires, the same ideals are everywhere apparent in the writings of the age, both sacred and profane; its atmosphere pervades both the statuary of Chartres and the Marian sermons and poems of St Bernard. France was discovering love; both courtly love and love of the Virgin Mary. It was the duty of the prelates and, above all, of the monks to sublimate carnal love and to canalize these emotive trends into the liturgies of the Church. About 1140 Peter the Venerable, Abbot of Cluny, introduced into the traditional hymnal the passages relating to the Nativity. In the soft radiance of lamps and candelabra, in clouds of incense, the sonorous Latin incantations took on the quality of a rite of coronation, the crowning of the Mother of God.

"I hail thee, Virgin Mary, spouse of the All-highest, mother of the gentle Lamb of God, who hast put to flight the powers of evil. Thou reignest in heaven and savest those on earth; men yearn towards thee and the evil spirits fear thee. Thou art the window, the door and the veil, the courtyard and the house, the temple, the earth, lily in thy virginity, rose by thy sufferings. Thou art the closed garden, the fountain of the garden that washes all who are defiled, purifies all who are corrupted and brings back life to the dead. Thou art the mistress of the ages, the hope, after God, of all generations, the king's house of rest and the abode of godhead. Thou art the star which, shining in the East, scatters the shadows of the West; the break of day; the light that knows no darkness. Thou, who didst engender Him who is our begetter, hast the joy of a mother who has well fulfilled her task, reconciled man with God. Pray, O Mother, the God whom thou didst bring into this world to forgive our sins that, after forgiving us, he may bestow on us grace and glory. Amen." The great Benedictine prayers invest the Virgin Mother with the majesty that inspired the art of the cathedrals. For the priests who devised its setting the Christmas festival solemnized in highest heaven, chanted by the choirs of angels, the first coming of Christ the King. And so the woman who had given birth to Him held an exalted place in the celestial hierarchy. It was from the store of symbolic names garnered by Abbot Peter that the first Marian iconology drew its vocabulary, while other metaphors—the garden enclosed, the orchard, the bed of sweet flowers, the tower of ivory—were taken from the Song of Songs. In the prayer that Dante puts into the mouth of St Bernard in the *Paradiso* we find a similar range of symbols.

> Thou Virgin Mother, daughter of thy Son,
> Humble and high beyond all other creatures,
> The limit fixed of the eternal counsel,
> Thou art the one who such nobility
> To human nature gave that its Creator
> Did not disdain to make himself its creature.
> Within thy womb rekindled was the love
> By warmth of which in the eternal peace
> After such wise this flower has germinated.
> Here unto us thou art a noonday torch
> Of charity, and below, in the world of mortals,
> Thou art the living fountainhead of hope.

As champion of the Queen of Heaven, St Bernard, who had entered the lists against the greatest churchmen of the day, now joined issue with the knights of the princely courts. Seeking to "convert" them, too, and lead them back to the way of holiness, he drew up the rule of a new religious order, the Templars. This was composed of converted warriors who, while remaining knights, had become monks, a *nova militia* who directed their arms against the enemies of Christ and their love towards Our Lady. St Bernard urged all the warriors of France to follow their king in a new crusade and enlist their restless energy under the banner of God. Likewise, he tried to orient the emotions celebrated in the literature in favor at the courts—love songs and romances—towards the path of mysticism. Stirred by his passionate appeal, some of the courtly poets underwent a conversion, supreme achievement of which in the field of literature was the famous romance of the Quest of the Holy Grail (c. 1200); the earliest version of it, written some years before the turn of the century, was *Le Conte del Graal* by Chrétien de Troyes. Whereas the heroes of earlier romances had practised a merely conventional religion, the Christianity of Perceval (the tale of whose adventures he composed some time before 1190) was a religion based on love of the Saviour, on penitence and prayer, and it extolled purity as the highest virtue. After the triumph of St Bernard young noblemen underwent the ceremony of dubbing and the ancient rite of initiation into knighthood as if it were indeed a sacrament. They came to it escorted by priests, prepared for it by a night of prayer in the oratory; a bath—a second baptism—washed them clean of sin, and then and only then could they join an order whose members practised the virtues of Christ, or were enjoined to practise them. For the victory of the Cistercian doctrines was only on the surface. It was by no means so easy as St Bernard thought to quell these young men's appetite for profane pleasures, for luxury and high living, for showy exploits in the lists or on the battlefield.

In any case Citeaux itself was following the trend of the times when the century drew to its close. It was common knowledge that the Cistercian abbeys were extremely wealthy. The White Monks had many sources of income—benefices, tithes and rents—while the menial tasks were performed by "serfs" recruited from the peasantry. Like feudal lords, the Cistercians lived on others' labor, and soon, tiring of the seclusion of the cloisters, they mingled in the life of the townsfolk. St Bernard might be outraged at the proposal that he should be an archbishop, but one of his monks had quitted the monastery to ascend the papal throne as Eugenius III. Other friars followed a similar path as the twelfth century ended; they wore the mitre, built cathedrals, took to study, and soon the order founded in Paris a daughter house where instruction was given in the humanities. At Toulouse the clergy chose for their bishop the abbot of Le Thoronet, a Cistercian monastery. This was Folquet of Marseilles, formerly a troubadour, and before long a new bishop's church was erected on the lines of those of the Ile-de-France. And at this same time the fact had to be faced that Citeaux had completely failed in its latest enterprise, the systematic eradication of heresy in the South.

the confines of the civilized world, Ireland, Scotland and Scandinavia still were barbarous countries peopled by nomad tribes of hunters and fishermen. England had no towns, nor had the forested parts of Germany. The lands of the Empire, where Charlemagne had now been canonized, were still in process of assimilating little by little Carolingian culture. All these regions lacked schools, or where they existed they had not yet fallen in line with the advanced ideas of the West. They knew nothing of the new liturgies celebrating the Divine Light and the Incarnation, nor had they yet been touched by the spirit of inquiry which led thinkers to seek out the truth and nourish their faith with understanding; choral singing was the main element of the curriculum. In any case the cathedral chapters were composed of members of the feudal nobility; the archbishops and canons of Lyons and of Arles were great lords ever ready for the fray, better trained in wielding arms than in using their brains. In these provinces the monasteries were the chief centers of religious life, but the monks confined themselves to liturgies in the Cluniac mode; when any new idea made its appearance it was usually sidetracked into some innocuous path. When Hildegard, Abbess of Bingen, wrote her *Liber divinorum operum* she took inspiration from an allegorical poem recently composed by a prelate of Chartres, but transmuted what she found in it into a tissue of incoherencies bathed in the apocalyptic atmosphere of the Beatus *Commentaries*. Similarly, when the Calabrian abbot, Joachim of Floris, took over Suger's exposition of the concordances between the Old and New Testaments he handled it in such a way that it dwindled into vague, messianic reveries. Here again we have evidence of a mentality that had failed to keep in step with the spirit of the age.

In other parts of Europe, however, the progressive ideas deriving from the Ile-de-France came up against trends of thought which, prompted by an intellectual evolution quite as active as that of the region around Paris, took a very different course. South of the Loire it was the spirit of the courts of chivalry that came in conflict with Gothic art. Aquitaine had never acquiesced in Carolingian overlordship and had doggedly resisted Pepin, Charlemagne and Charles the Bald. It had never accepted their conceptions of a learned clergy, of church schools, and of the fusion of the spiritual and the temporal *potestas* in the person of the Frankish king, but

had continued to keep religion and life in separate compartments: on the one hand the lofty ideal of the cloister, on the other the pleasures of the fashionable world. During the eleventh century Aquitaine was the region most affected by the ecclesiastical reform promoted by Pope Gregory VII. The religious communities were freed from state control, monks and churchmen differentiated from the lay nobility more sharply than in the past, the former dedicated to chastity, the latter spending their days in feats of arms and love-making. The princes of Aquitaine did not think themselves invested with any sacred function and took little or no interest in their religious duties, while the members of their courts trusted to the prayers of the monks for the salvation of their souls, and hoped by generous alms-giving to earn sufficient merit to justify a life of pleasure-seeking. They enjoyed hunting and warfare no less than did the knights of France, but they lived in cities where the Roman tradition of urbanity had not declined to the same extent and they could still relish the more refined joys of civilized life. About 1100 a Duke of Aquitaine made the first love-songs in the French tongue, adjusting to the melodies of Gregorian chants verses in praise of his ladylove, and all the young men at his court followed suit. They invented the love game in which the young man idolizes his lord's wife and transfers to her the loyalty, services and vassalage he owes his lord. This code of courtly manners developed in an aristocracy whose emotions were less bridled than they were north of the Loire by the Church, which here kept strictly to its cloisters and ritual devotions. It gained ground in the region of Toulouse, in Provence and later in Italy. The nobility of all the provinces that were truly French finished by adopting it, if not without twinges of remorse, in the second half of the twelfth century. King Louis VII had married the heiress of the dukes of Aquitaine, but her frivolity displeased him; the monks in his entourage, Suger to begin with, convinced him that it was of diabolic origin and persuaded him to divorce her.

Eleanor of Aquitaine soon found another husband, Henry Plantagenet, King of England, who was already possessed of the continental inheritance of Anjou and still held Normandy. After his marriage the king extended his domain over a long chain of territories covering about half the kingdom of France. Determined to outdo the Capetian king, he bade the intellectuals of his court devise an aesthetic capable of competing with that of Paris. Indifferent to faith and intellectual problems, this new aesthetic aimed at giving pleasure and stimulating the imagination. Hence its combination of "courtesy," a speciality of Aquitaine, with the *matière de Bretagne*, meaning the English idiom. The royal Abbey of Malmesbury—British equivalent of Saint-Denis—near the Welsh border was the repository of a wealth of legendary lore (including the Arthurian cycle), fructified by the Celtic imagination. From it the writers at the court of Henry II drew the themes of their romances: fabulous adventures of knights errant slaying dragons in the perilous quest of some fair lady. The tragic tale of Tristan and Iseult challenged the French martial epics describing the exploits of helmeted bishops and Charlemagne's valiant knights; challenged, too, the mystic chivalry of Perceval. The art of France came up against a similar resistance in the west. The cathedral of Angers, while utilizing crossed ogival arches, retained the massive structure of the Romanesque churches of Poitou. In point of fact the aesthetic of the Plantagenet domain never achieved an architectural style of its own. Its art was almost always confined to the poetic field and, except in English book illuminations, whose free-flowing line was frankly opposed to the stateliness of the Chartres statuary, rarely found visual expression. The only monumental illustrations of the romances which were written for the princes of western France are to be seen in Italian cathedrals. Characters from the Tale of Troy figure in a mosaic pavement at Bitonto, and the Knights of the Round Table on a tympanum at Modena. These can be accounted for by the fact that the Italian élite were attracted by the culture of the princely courts of northern France and that in Italian cities the cathedral, heir of the ancient basilica, was as much a civic as a religious edifice. For here, far more than in France, the cathedral was the common property of all the citizens, it was quite literally "their" house.

On the southeast of Latin Christendom other factors, perhaps more deeply rooted, in any case more active and stimulated by the growth of commerce in the Mediterranean area, combated the influence of the Ile-de-France. Here the relapse of western Christendom into the barbarism of the early Middle Ages had never quite extinguished the towns

and they had soon recovered their vitality. The Germans streaming down through the Brenner Pass were startled to find them so powerful. The communes had driven back the feudal barons into the poverty-stricken castles of the countryside, brought to heel the bishop and his priests, vanquished Frederick Barbarossa and carried back in triumph to Milan the eagles of the Empire. Within their city walls arose a type of culture which, as in Aquitaine, though emancipated from Church control, was tributary to the schools. For the Italian schools were not ecclesiastical, nor did they base their education on theology; any Italian youth who wished to study it went to Paris. In this part of Italy, in Pavia and above all at the University of Bologna, jurisprudence was the chief discipline. It was in Bologna that at the end of the eleventh century Justinian's *Digest* was rediscovered and henceforth this text held the same place in the local curriculum as that of the Scriptures in the *studia* of the Ile-de-France. For its interpretation the same methods of dialectical analysis were applied as those employed for elucidating the Decretals of canon law, and in his *Concordia discordantium canonum* Gratian (c. 1140) took the same intellectual approach as that of Abelard. But this discipline was unconcerned with religion and intended solely to provide a corps of jurists for the service of the Emperor and the cities where they practised. Further south in Italy, around the provinces formerly ruled by Byzantium and Islam, other forms of education emerged; they too were of a temporal order, relating to the body, not the soul. In these schools medicine and astrology bulked large, and, algebra and astronomy being needed for drawing up reliable horoscopes, there was an intensive study of translations of Hippocrates, Galen and Aristotle. Neglecting Aristotle's works on logic, the professors read his *Meterologica* and sought to learn from him what were the links between the four elements of the cosmos and the "humors" of man. In Italy, now that the communes were in the saddle, the curriculum of the schools centered on practical life.

In South European cities the Church no longer sought to base its teachings on logical argument: it did not preach; it chanted. None the less the advance of civilization was taking effect on the mentality of an élite in the larger towns. For soon the rites and ceremonies of church services ceased to satisfy the knights, lawyers and businessmen, all of whom had a feeling of guilt vis-à-vis their Maker. Anxious to save their souls, they sought for spiritual nourishment. No longer finding this in the cathedral, they listened eagerly to the itinerant preachers who delivered sermons at street corners and in public squares. These men, anyhow, spoke their language, they had a message to deliver. Many of them were renegades, former members of the clergy who had left the church, feeling ill at ease among the canons, or else had failed to win admittance to the exalted circles mainly reserved to sons of wealthy parents. Tempted neither by the cloister nor by the hermit's cell, they felt constrained to preach the word of God—usually in an aggressive manner, for the bishops hounded them down remorselessly.

Most of them preached penitence. Behind the heretical movement lay a desire for the reform of the Church and this—the preachers stressed the point—linked up with the reforming zeal of the great Pope Gregory. The cathedral prelates were unworthy, corrupted by worldliness and luxury. What value had sacraments administered by their soiled hands, the chants rising from their tainted lips? The people had need of efficacious rites; let them, then, expel the sinful priests and restore to the Church its spiritual mission. Given the social unrest in the towns, such words had an immediate appeal. Would not the act of stripping the bishop of his temporal power bring freedom to the community? Surely, too, the rule of apostolic poverty justified insurrections of this order. In 1146 Arnold of Brescia, a canon regular who had studied at Paris and one of the leaders of the reformist movement in Italy, set up a commune in Rome, basing his campaign against the wealthy Curia on the poverty of Christ. Nine years later, after being denounced as a heretic for bidding the prelates "lead the life of Jesus," he was hanged and his body burnt. If Arnold's campaign had a political tinge, this gradually died out as the cult of "holy poverty" gained ground in the middle class; the rich merchant of Lyons Peter Waldo was far from being a leader of revolt. Waldo had a translation made of the Gospels into Provençal and learnt from them that as a rich man he was excluded from the kingdom of God. So he sold all his possessions, gave the money to the poor and, with a view to assuring municipal independence for his fellow citizens, took to preaching. But since he was a layman, the archbishop forbade him to speak about religion, sentenced him (in 1180) and had the sentence confirmed by the pope. His disciples, the Waldensians, had to go into hiding. Even so this clandestine sect, in revolt against the established Church, attracted a large following—chiefly of businessmen, cattle merchants and weavers—in the cities, country towns and villages of the Alpine region, Provence and Italy.

Meanwhile, in the Toulouse district, other sectaries were making many converts to a doctrine which, though invoking the name of Christ, differed radically from Christianity. Here the Catholic Church was openly challenged by a rival church, that of the Cathars. The way to this revolt against the establishment had been prepared, early in the twelfth century, by such unorthodox preachers as Peter of Bruys and Henry of Lausanne. They too began by violently attacking the worldly lives of the clergy. The bishops called them Manichaeans, and it is clear that in their championship of poverty and purity they tended to stress the antinomy between the spiritual and carnal principles and to represent the world as the scene of an endless conflict between Good and Evil, sequel of the primal war in heaven. Their teachings were readily accepted in a region where, more than elsewhere, the layman rarely came in touch with the servants of God. The fact that in the latter half of the century this dualism was explicitly formulated and crystallized into a rigid doctrinal system was due both to the influence of the Crusades and to closer contacts with the Balkans by way of trade. The Greek word "Cathar" made its first appearance in 1163, when it was applied to the members of this sect. By this time they were very numerous, probably more numerous than the orthodox Catholics in some districts. Twenty years before, alarmed by their growth, St Bernard had thundered against them—but in vain. The victor on this occasion was not the Cistercian abbot but a newcomer from the East, Nicetas, bishop of the heretical sect of the Bogomils, who installed four bishops in Languedoc and one in northern Italy. It was now that the chapter general of Cîteaux received a call for aid from Count Raymond of Toulouse. All his noble vassals, he said, were being contaminated and a whole community in the Albi region had broken with the Church and embraced the rival religion.

Here there was no question of a mere deviation; rather, of a new dogma. We shall never have a clear idea of its tenets, so ruthlessly was Catharism exterminated by the inquisitors of the next century.

They destroyed its records, wiped out all trace of it. However, from the manuals issued for the guidance of the inquisitors we can learn some basic facts. The Cathars were dualists, believing that two supreme powers or principles exist: a god of light and the spirit, a god of darkness and the flesh, perpetually competing for the governance of the world. Man is involved in the combat, and in it his future is at stake. For if he wishes to have access to the light after he dies, instead of being reincarnated in a fleshly body, he must co-operate in the victory of the "light principle," that is to say shun everything in which Satan has a part, reject money, nourish himself with the least impure aliments, eat no flesh and refrain from carnal intercourse. For procreating favors the triumph of the material and adds recruits to the Satanic host. In practice only a few Cathars, the so-called Perfecti, were capable of this total ascesis. These men, "vessels of election," had the power of ensuring the salvation of weaker brethren and, by the imposition of hands, even *in extremis*, of impregnating them with the Spirit. Familiar with intercession of this type, the inhabitants of Aquitaine felt no qualms about delegating to others the vocations of poverty and chastity and entrusting to the ritual gestures of these specialists in salvation the care of their souls, while they themselves enjoyed with a clear conscience the good things of this world. The "Perfects" had this advantage, that in their lives they gave a shining example of self-imposed poverty and that they were less hypocritical and exacted less from the people than the clergy. Hence they seemed far better qualified as intercessors between man and God. Noble troubadours and wealthy merchants often called them in, on their deathbeds, to administer the Cathar rite of *Consolamentum*, or "baptism of the Spirit," and many of the wives of the lords of Aquitaine in their declining years formed "Communities of Perfect Life."

We may be sure that few of these men and women had any clear notion of the radical antinomy between the doctrine of the "Perfects" and orthodox Catholicism. For the exponents of the Bogomil dualism had taken over the terminology and some of the symbols used by the Catholic clergy—to such effect that the transition from the anti-episcopal diatribes of the preachers to the paradoxes of Cathar dogma passed unnoticed. None the less that dogma repudiated the hierarchical orders defined by Dionysius, his theory of progression from the Source and ultimate return, and indeed the whole idea of Creation. For how could matter, intrinsically evil, emanate from a God who was the principle of goodness? The Cathars also rejected the doctrine of the Incarnation; they saw, it seems, in Jesus only an angel sent on earth by the God of Light, and justified this view by the opening pages of the Gospel of St John. How, they asked, could the divine illumination have submerged itself in the darkness of the flesh and taken form in a woman's womb? How, then, endorse the cult of Mary? They rejected, too, the notion of redemption. How could the God of Light have suffered in his flesh, what value could be assigned to the pangs of a mortal body? Thus the "Perfects" broke completely with the ideas embodied in Suger's Saint-Denis, with the doctrine of the Trinity and the iconography of the cathedrals.

At the end of the twelfth century the addicts of diverse forms of heresy, the Cathars and the Waldensians (also known as Vaudois) who dispensed with priests and practised their purifying rites in secret, the many obscure sects that flourished in the south and in the cultured circles of the courts—all alike set up a solid resistance to the ideology of the schools of Paris and the concepts of the cathedral builders. But heresy went further; it imperilled the unity of Christendom. Expressing as it did the troubled mental climate of the age, it came to be the prime concern of the rulers of the Church. The best of the monks, the Cistercians, had failed in their crusading mission; the Abbot of Citeaux had to confess defeat. It behooved the Roman Church to use all the weapons in its armory. Why not those of art? It was already used in Italy in the service of orthodox propaganda. In 1138 Guglielmo of Lucca confronted those who doubted the efficacy of His sacrifice with an image of Christ crucified, and in the choir of Santa Maria in Trastevere, in Rome, a mosaic was set up celebrating the triumph of the Mother of God. Both works proclaimed the truth of the Incarnation, just as Benedetto Antelami's *Deposition from the Cross* (1178) affirmed that of the Redemption. At Arles, in the porch of Saint-Gilles, all the arguments for the True Faith were figured forth dramatically. Thus at the end of the twelfth century all the possibilities of visual persuasion were being exploited in the Romanesque art of southern Europe. It was, however, the art of the Gothic cathedrals that now became what was perhaps the Church's most efficacious ally in the war on heresy.

THE ART OF THE WEST

The success of the cathedral schools of Neustria had a profound and stimulating influence on the evolution of twelfth-century culture. All the same the art language based on the transcription of the new theology into visual terms did not hold its own unchallenged. We find signs of an insidious penetration of scholastic values into the world of art, though this process was very gradual and is often hard to trace.

Most of the students in the Parisian schools came from the region between the Loire and the Rhine, and from England. The new aesthetic made headway earliest in these provinces, but never wholly dominated them. Thus the art of the illuminated book was little if at all affected; it formed a domain apart, untouched by the prevailing trend. This was because illumination was a less public art and relatively immune to the pressure of official propaganda. The illustrator of manuscripts was surrounded by much older works and took inspiration from them. Also, during this period, he was more controlled than other artists by the monks, and the abbey schools were becoming more and more conservative, less disposed to welcome new ideas. For them, far longer than in the outside world, God remained "the Invisible" and artists working in monastic scriptoria sought above all to interpret in line and color their inner vision and their reveries.

As a result of the Scandinavian invasions in the tenth century, of the intensification of maritime traffic which had preceded them and continued after them, and, most notably, of the Norman conquest, a close cultural association developed between England and Western France. In this part of Europe the manuscript painters kept to the Carolingian tradition; they modeled their work on books that were illuminated in the Franco-insular style, in which two trends were intermingled. The first, which triumphed about 1150 at Hénin-Liétard, at Saint-Amand and Valenciennes, derived from the "renaissance" spirit active in the palatine school, its purposive revival of the imperial art of Antiquity. This humanist tradition gave rise to monumental figures of Evangelists and Doctors of the Church and Crucifixions stamped with a classical serenity. A second, very different art came from the British Isles, where it had taken refuge in the tenth century. Winchester was the chief scene of the flowering of this art of free fancy. It abounds in pictures of weird monsters, in scenes of hell and the apocalyptic visions described in Revelations, and its line has all the suppleness and emotive dynamism of the drawings in the Utrecht Psalter. In representations of human figures this line is disciplined, quite in the classical spirit; but it runs free in animal and vegetable forms, weaving them into flowing arabesques and geometric convolutions.

GOSPEL BOOK OF HÉNIN-LIÉTARD: ST MATTHEW, 12TH CENTURY.
FOLIO 22 VERSO, MS 14, I, BIBLIOTHÈQUE MUNICIPALE, BOULOGNE-SUR-MER.

74

SACRAMENTARY OF SAINT-AMAND: CRUCIFIXION, SECOND HALF OF THE 12TH CENTURY.
FOLIO 58 VERSO, MS 108, BIBLIOTHÈQUE MUNICIPALE, VALENCIENNES.

UTRECHT PSALTER (COPY): ILLUSTRATION FOR PSALM XLIII. LATE 12TH CENTURY (?).
FOLIO 76, MS LAT. 8846, BIBLIOTHÈQUE NATIONALE, PARIS.

EADWINE PSALTER: ILLUSTRATION FOR PSALM XLIII, ABOUT 1150.
MS R. 17.1, TRINITY COLLEGE LIBRARY, CAMBRIDGE.

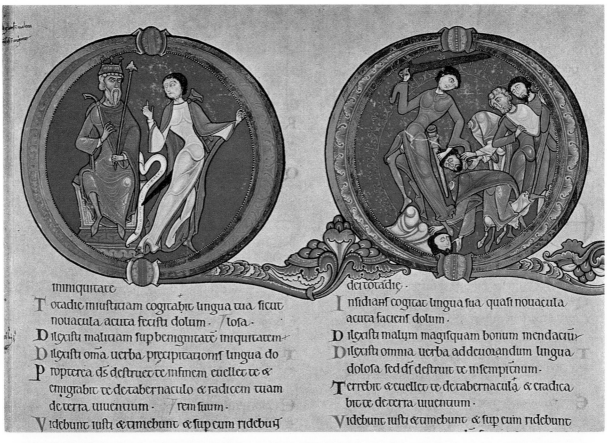

in iniquitate

Tota die iniusticiam cogitabit lingua tua sicut
nouacula acuta fecisti dolum · /Iosa·

Dilexisti maliciam sup benignitatem iniquitatem ·

Dilexisti oma uerba precipitationis lingua do

Propterea ds destruet te infinem euellet te &
emigrabit te detabernaculo & radicem tuam
de terra uiuentium · /rem suum·

Videbunt iusti & timebunt & sup eum ridebunt

de tota die ·

Insidias cogitat lingua sua quasi nouacula
acuta faciens dolum ·

Dilexisti malum magisquam bonum mendaciu

Dilexisti omnia uerba addeuorandum lingua
dolosa sed ds destruit te insempiturnum ·

Terrebit & euellet te detabernacula & eradica
bit te deterra uiuentium ·

Videbunt iusti & timebunt & sup eum ridebunt

BIBLE OF HENRY OF BLOIS: DOEG THE EDOMITE SLAYING THE PRIESTS OF NOB. SECOND HALF OF THE 12TH CENTURY.
VOL. III, FOLIO 16 RECTO, CATHEDRAL LIBRARY, WINCHESTER.

E la beste est prise eodlu le faul pphete ki fist sig   sut mil uist en te estaunk de fu. coest eus uist en lur
nes deuaur lu n les auel el mes ceus l tremt

APOCALYPSE: THE DRAGON WITH SEVEN HEADS CAST DOWN FROM HEAVEN. ST ALBANS, ABOUT 1230.
MS R. 16.2, TRINITY COLLEGE LIBRARY, CAMBRIDGE.

ENAMELLED FUNERARY PLAQUE ALLEGEDLY FROM THE TOMB OF GEOFFREY PLANTAGENET (1113-1151) IN LE MANS CATHEDRAL.
12TH CENTURY. MUSÉE DE TESSÉ, LE MANS.

ITALY

In the twelfth century churchmen, knights, merchants, even peasants could travel much more freely than in the past and these journeys, encounters and exchanges of ideas did something to reduce the barriers between the various provinces of Christian Europe. All the same they remained shut up, to some extent, in watertight compartments. If we were asked to make a "map of culture" for the period—an almost hopeless task, given the gaps in our information—we should have to begin by delineating a network of interlocking frontiers, a complex of fragmentated units, refractory in many cases to any outside influence, a many-faceted pattern of regional particularities. It would, however, be possible to discern in this medley of conflicting ideologies and mores a clear-cut dividing line corresponding to the political cleavage of which all the men of the time who gave thought to such matters were acutely conscious. Running north and south this line separated the Kingdom (that is to say France and the western zone of Latin Christendom) from what still survived of the Empire: Germany, Italy and the satellite states, politically and culturally united since the tenth century under a single government.

During this period the king of Germany became as a matter of course Roman Emperor. When Frederick Barbarossa sought to restore the Empire to the position it had occupied in its glorious past, he made a point of asserting the imperial prerogative at Besançon and Arles, in Lombardy and Tuscany, and declared himself the heir of Charlemagne. This may explain the ascendancy of the Carolingian aesthetic in these parts of Europe and its resistance to the blandishments of the royal art of France. For there could be no denying that the art of the emperors, descendants of Charlemagne and Otto the Great, was in the lineage of the art of the Caesars. Thus all the new churches built in Germany, Lombardy, Tuscany and Rome retained the proportions of the ancient basilicas. In the interior there were the same arcades, the same system of lighting, the same timber ceilings. There were also frescoes and often, under the triumphal arch, an image of the Crucifixion, symbol of the triumph of the Church. In most cases the façades were very soberly adorned. However, the new affluence of the Tuscan cities, due to their sea-borne trade, commercial enterprise and the manufacture of costly imitations of Oriental luxury wares, led them to decorate the fronts of their churches. Indeed this desire to flaunt their opulence often gave rise to an excess of ornamentation, an over-lavish use of color, a plethora of sculpture. There are many points in common between the churches of Lucca and the imperial art of Rome and Ravenna: notably the façades with their curtain of tracery fretting the western light, pediments and long colonnades.

FAÇADE OF THE CHURCH OF SAN MICHELE IN FORO, LUCCA. BEGUN ABOUT 1210.

FAÇADE OF BAMBERG CATHEDRAL, FOUNDED BY HENRY II. 1004-1012 (RESTORED ABOUT 1081 AND AGAIN IN 1185).

INTERIOR OF THE ALL SAINTS CHAPEL, REGENSBURG. 12TH CENTURY.

MOSAICS

In the course of the thirteenth century the art of France forced its way into Italy, this incursion being promoted, firstly, by the Holy See, which saw in the aesthetic of the University the most effective vehicle of Catholic theology and, secondly, by the religious Orders, its faithful exponents: the Cistercians and after them the Mendicants. None the less, the scope of this French influence was necessarily limited since it came up against two forms of culture which in the course of many centuries had solidly established themselves in Italy: that of imperial Rome and that of Byzantium.

The Germanic invasions had swept through Italy from end to end, brushing aside the figurative and humanist traditions of Roman art and imposing an art of jewelers and engravers, the barbarous geometry and weird animal forms of the Nordic belt-buckles. But a considerable part of Italy had held out against the intruders and incorporation in Charlemagne's empire. Latium was never more than a weakly held fringe of it; Venice and all the south kept their independence. These regions remained tied up with the East, and this association had been growing closer since the tenth century, now that the sea routes were being swept clear of pirates. That is why at the time when work was beginning on Notre-Dame in Paris the Doges of Venice still elected for a "Greek" decoration in St Mark's, and the Norman kings of Sicily did likewise for the walls of their palaces, oratories and cathedrals.

The Byzantine church was a habitation of the divine. Its façades were left severely plain and the aesthetic effort of its builders was concentrated on the interior, where mosaics spangling the shadows with flakes of living light conjured up visions of the Celestial City. The makers of the mosaics of Palermo and Monreale—and, following them, those of the Baptistery of Florence and the Monastery of the Santi Quattro Coronati in Rome—adopted the narrative form of presentation favored by the Duecento artists, but—this was a new development—couched it in the idiom of the then current Oriental iconography. The subjects are Gospel scenes and tales culled from the Apocrypha. Yet here, too, the logical spirit of the age makes itself felt; the settings of the figures of Christ's childhood and Passion are given a mathematical precision, space is carefully organized and each group of scenes boldly demarcated by a frame.

THE NATIVITY, 1140-1143. MOSAIC IN LA MARTORANA (CHURCH OF SANTA MARIA DELL'AMMIRAGLIO), PALERMO.

ΗΒΑΗΦΩΡΟΣ

THE ENTRY OF CHRIST INTO JERUSALEM, 1143. MOSAIC IN THE SANCTUARY, CAPPELLA PALATINA, PALERMO.

CHRIST PANTOCRATOR AND THE VIRGIN AND CHILD WITH ANGELS, APOSTLES AND SAINTS. 12TH-13TH CENTURY.
MOSAIC IN THE CENTRAL APSE OF THE CATHEDRAL, MONREALE (SICILY).

THE VIRGIN AND THE APOSTLES, DETAIL. 12TH-13TH CENTURY. APSE MOSAIC IN THE CATHEDRAL, TORCELLO (VENICE).

2

ROMANESQUE RESISTANCES

There were several factors telling against the rise of Gothic art, most active of them being the monastic tradition. Until the first quarter of the thirteenth century the monastery had played a leading role in the cultural evolution of the West, and the triumph of Cîteaux fell far short of eclipsing the ancient Benedictine style. The Benedictine monks held an exalted status in the social hierarchy since it was their sacred task to celebrate day by day and hour by hour the praise of God in rites invested with the utmost pomp and dignity. In England, which had been Christianized originally by the disciples of St Benedict, the monastery still was closely linked up with the cathedral and (as in Carolingian times) it was regarded as the cornerstone of the ecclesiastic edifice in the German provinces and the lands near the Slav frontier. But the regions in which its ascendancy was most pronounced were those which had come under the direct influence of Cluny in its heyday: Burgundy, southern Gaul, Catalonia and the fringe of Christendom which, starting from the Compostela pilgrim road, had widened out into the heart of Spain.

Linked together by a network of confraternities and daughter houses, these abbeys and priories were extremely wealthy. They held a secure place in the feudal system, owned large estates and had troops at their disposal; they levied tithes and land taxes, administered justice, had thriving villages in their domains and, along with the cathedral chapters, the monks who lived in them ranked as the aristocracy of the Church. Aging nobles often retired to them to end their days in peace and preparation for the after-life. They sent there those of their sons who seemed inapt for the profession of arms, so that they could pray for the welfare of the line, without falling short of the high estate of leisured ease to which it had pleased God to call them. However, the feudal barons were always wrangling with these institutions, accusing them of unfair competition and of infringing on their seigniorial rights. They harassed the abbots and priors with all sorts of petty vexations and chicaneries, and made difficulties about handing over to them, without reservations, the lands and peasants that, generation after generation, members of the nobility had donated to the monastery on their deathbeds. But though the barons pressed their claims so vigorously that they usually obtained compensation or a partition of these donations, they still were lavish in their gifts to the monastery. For most knights held land in fee from the abbot or prior, had done homage to him, owed him fealty and rallied round him at sessions of the feudal court. Moreover all of them revered this House of Worship to which they could delegate their chief religious duties; this place where their forefathers were buried and one day they would sleep beside them. On the anniversary of a man's death a memorial service was held in which prayers were made for his soul, ensuring his felicity in the next world. Also, the monastery church contained holy relics to which the populace *en masse* did obeisance on feast-days, which at certain seasons were carried in solemn procession across the countryside to ensure the fertility of the soil, and contact with which cured diseases. The monasteries were in fact organisms of collective intercession on which a whole province depended for its salvation. Everywhere, but most persistently in southern Europe, laymen committed their hope of a glorious resurrection to the good offices of the monastic community.

In a largely illiterate world the monasteries were oases of culture, in which books were preserved, studied and copied. But this culture was hampered by a host of antiquated regulations and in the period we are here considering its scope became still narrower. The spirit of monasticism is clearly reflected in its music. Revolving in a closed circle of harmonies and melodies, the chants accompanying the never-ceasing prayers of the monks had a somewhat stupefying effect on the mentality of the congregation. Their thoughts were not encouraged to rove in new directions, and kept to the measured rhythms of the liturgic chants, whose cycle corresponded to that of the seasons. The contrast between the rapid tempo of urban life and the stagnation of the countryside was paralleled by that between the venturous cathedral schools of Neustria and the static traditionalism of monastic culture.

Places of collective purification, readying men for the Last Judgment, the abbeys and priories served an eschatological end, for they were always awaiting Christ's Second Coming. This is why visions of the Apocalypse bulk so large in the iconography of their churches and Beatus's *Commentaria* always figured in their libraries. In these sanctuaries men were trained to face calmly and courageously the great catastrophes which were to precede the End of Time. They contained images of the dreaded Horsemen of the Apocalypse, carriers of the scourge of God, looming up on the horizon. On one of the capitals of Saint-Nectaire the Destroying Angel carries three arrows representing the three things most feared by the peasantry: war, famine, sudden death. Monastic art, however, centers primarily on the figure of the Son of Man, encircled by rays of dazzling celestial light. On the Angoulême façade we see Christ rising from the world of men in His Ascension and descending in glory for His final appearance on earth at the Last Day, proclaiming the death of Time, the triumph of eternal life in a world beyond the world.

In its inquiries into the scheme of things monastic thought was largely guided by visions of the ineffable, and moved in an imaginary realm. Hence the strong vein of fantasy in medieval sculpture, as well as in the illuminated books. Many of the themes relate to myths culled from *Bestiaries*, and are treated so esoterically that their symbolism is as dark to us today as it must have been to their contemporaries. What is the significance of the fights between men and animals on the portal of San Pietro of Spoleto? Where find a clue to the enigmatic reliefs which the Irish monks who settled in Regensburg in the twelfth century set up on each side of the entrance to their church?

ROMANESQUE RESISTANCES

1. The Destroying Angel, detail of a capital in the church of Saint-Nectaire (Puy-de-Dôme), France. 12th century.

2. Christ in Majesty, detail of the frieze over the door of the church of San Pedro de Moarbes (Palencia), Spain. 12th century.

3. The Trinity, detail of the doorway of the church of Santo Domingo at Soria, Spain. 13th century.

4. West front of Notre-Dame-la-Grande at Poitiers. 11th-12th century.

5. Bas-reliefs on the façade of the church of San Pietro at Spoleto, Italy. 12th century.

6. Dome of the collegiate church of Santa Maria la Mayor at Toro (Zamora), Spain. Begun in 1160.

7. Portal of the church of St James (Schotten-kirche) at Regensburg, Germany. 12th century.

4

5

5

94

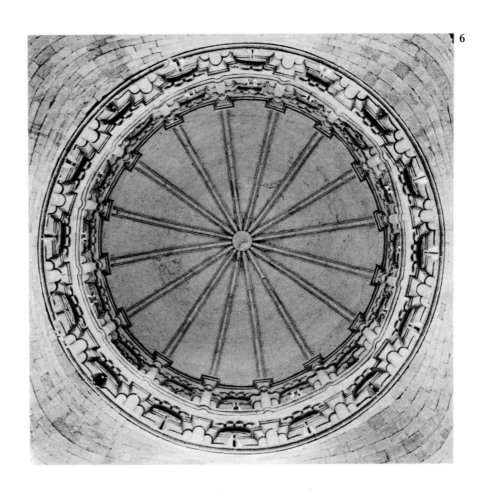

II

THE AGE OF REASON
1190-1250

THE CATHOLIC REPRESSION

At the close of the twelfth century the Church was a beleaguered fortress. Some of the outer bastions had been stormed, the last lines of defence were but precariously held, and the most active and alarming of its enemies was heresy. But this was not the only danger. Another, more insidious threat stemmed from the rapid advance of learning which, in the school of Paris in particular, was giving rise to daring speculations, often of a subversive nature. As a result of closely analysing the works of Dionysius and pondering on the mystery of the Trinity and the Creation, Amalric of Bena, a teacher of philosophy at the university of Paris, came to think and taught his pupils that since "all is one and God is all," every Christian was a member of the body of Christ and as such immune from sin. Knowing himself "possessed" by God, he could indulge in a life of joy and freedom. Needless to say, this doctrine was greatly to the taste of the young noblemen and poets of the courts (hence its prompt success), but it also implied that a priesthood was superfluous (hence its drastic condemnation by the church authorities).

Meanwhile Parisian teachers were turning more and more to the pagan philosophy of Aristotle. In 1205 the pope himself sent some of them to Constantinople to study Greek thought at its source, while at Toledo the teams of translators which had already produced a version of the *Organon* had moved on to the master's *Physics* and *Metaphysics*. The eyes of theological students and teachers were being opened to a body of logically argued and demonstrated theses which provided a rational, coherent explanation of the universe, but nevertheless relied on premises that were patently incompatible with those of Holy Writ. There was, then, a danger that the very men whose duty it was to uphold the dogmas of the Church and to do away with heresy might let themselves be lured from the Faith by the seductions of these pagan works. The first symptoms of doubt, the first deviations, manifested themselves at the very time when the rapid growth of affluence and an urge to make the most of it were tending to undermine, insensibly, the established social order. Based on a monastic ideal of withdrawal, and given form at a time when the population consisted of backward peasants and uncultured warriors, the structure of the Church was ill-adjusted to the contemporary world and its aspirations. If unity was to be regained a drastic revision was obviously called for, the structure had to be tightened up. In the result the Church was given a monarchical, not to say totalitarian form, centered on the Holy See and, specifically, on the personality of a very able pope, Innocent III.

For over a century the papacy had been consolidating and extending its power. It had successfully defied emperors, and the jurists of the Curia had formulated a system of theocracy by which the pope was vested with an *auctoritas* superior to that of any temporal power. He claimed a right of moral jurisdiction over the whole world, sent his legates everywhere and sought to keep the bishops under his direct control. Elected pope in 1198 when he was only thirty-eight, Innocent III brought this long effort to a successful conclusion. Born of a noble family, he was a well-educated man, had studied law at Bologna (in the Italian style), then theology in Paris (Neustrian style). He was the first pope categorically to declare himself not only a successor of St Peter, but Christ's vicegerent on earth—in other words a king of kings, *rex regum*, who ranked above all princes and was their judge. On the day of his coronation he proclaimed: "It is to me that Jesus said 'I will give unto thee the keys of the kingdom of heaven: and whatsoever thou shalt bind on earth shall be bound in heaven.' See him, then, this servant of the Lord for what he is: vicar of Christ, and successor of St Peter. He stands midway between God and man, less great than God, greater than man." The pope accordingly set out to assert his feudal suzerain rights over all the states of Europe

—and he nearly succeeded in this attempt. Assured of his supremacy, he held at the end of his reign an ecumenical council at the Lateran which played the same part in medieval Christendom as the Council of Trent was to play in sixteenth-century Europe. Innocent clearly defined his program: it was "to stamp out heresy and to fortify faith, but also to reform men's morals, extirpate vices, implant virtues, remove excesses. Also to allay disputes, establish peace, repudiate tyranny, and to cause the Truth to prevail everywhere, for all."

So now the Church was mustering its forces, consolidating its position, expelling foreign bodies. A previous Council in 1179 had enacted that all impure persons affected with purulent diseases, madmen and those possessed by devils were to be segregated in lazar-houses, so that good Christians might not be infected. Innocent's Council followed this up by ordering all Jews to wear a distinctive circular badge so that they might not be confused with Christians. Next, the Church, mindful of Catholic unity, launched an attack on schismatics (in 1204 the Crusaders captured Constantinople), but above all on heretics, the major danger. In 1209 the pope proclaimed the same indulgences for a crusade to Languedoc, for the suppression of the Albigenses, as for crusades to the Holy Land. In the struggle to achieve world power, characteristic of Innocent's pontificate, the Church knew it could count no longer on the monks.

For the old monastic orders had fallen into disrepute. They were the targets of ribald jests at the banquets of the knights. The didactic poems written in their language for the French nobility at the close of the twelfth century are full of criticisms of Cluny, Cîteaux and the Chartreuse, where, entrenched in their cloisters, the monks led self-indulgent lives and behaved "like vulgar tradesmen at their junketings." The knightly orders, Templars and Hospitallers, were viewed more favorably. They, anyhow, went out into the world, risked their lives and promoted, after their fashion, one of the ideals of chivalry; they stood for a Church Militant. None the less the religious movements which now were giving rise to new congregations sponsored a life no longer centered on the clash of arms, on knightly jousts and tourneys, but on brotherly love. The Imitation of Christ in his care for the poor was the guiding principle of the new Order of the Holy Ghost, and

the Order of the Trinitarians devoted itself to the liberation of Christian captives. These Orders won the admiration of the populace at large, and they alone challenged with success the heretic sects. Innocent III was well aware of this when he re-admitted to the Church certain sects dedicated to the rule of poverty and some offshoots of the Waldensian heresy. He welcomed into the fold the Pauperes Catholici and the Order of the Humiliati and encouraged laic penances. But it was left to two great evangelists, the two "Princes" of whom Dante speaks, to lead to Christ the Church, his bride; two men whom "Providence ordained in her behoof/ Who on this side and that should be her guide": St Francis of Assisi and St Dominic.

In 1205 the hills of Languedoc had not as yet been scoured by troops of Parisian horsemen slaughtering, in the name of Christ, the Albigensian heretics. This was the year when Innocent III received a visit from the bishop of Osma (in Spain) and Dominic, sub-prior of his chapter. On their way to Rome these two men had traversed the domain of Catharism, then in its hour of triumph, and had met at Montpellier the disheartened papal legates. The reasons for the Catholic defeat were evident to them: the lax morals and indecent wealth of the clergy. The Spanish prelates informed the pope that "to shut the mouths of evil men it is needful for churchmen to behave and talk in accordance with the example of their Master, to practise humility, to travel on foot without gold or silver, in short to copy faithfully the apostles' way of life." The bishop and his canons told the pope of their resolve to renounce the pomp and luxury which all the prelates of the West had flaunted since the days of Charlemagne, rich garments and the insignia of temporal power. Their plan was to return to the heresy-ridden lands and preach the Gospel, in truly evangelical fashion, as poor men "without purse and scrip." The pope wished them Godspeed. In the Narbonne region, at Pamiers, Lavaur and Fanjeaux, they engaged in public disputations with the "Perfects" and everyone could see that the envoys of the Church were, like their adversaries, without weapons, wives or wealth in any form. There were jousts of eloquence, for Dominic and his companions were schoolmen, intellectuals. Heresy had vanquished the men of the cloister and now the men of the schools entered the fray. They had marshalled in advance their arguments, in the *langue d'oc*, the language of the people, and this time Catharism was to be attacked on dogmatic grounds, refuted by theological premises. These debates were attended by members of the nobility and middle class who, as in tournaments, decided on the winner. Dominic alone remained in France and it was now that he founded, at Prouille, near Toulouse, the first nunnery, a refuge for women converted from heresy, as an antidote for the "conventicles" where ladies of the region made retreats under the strict régime of Cathar perfectionism. He imposed on the nuns the rule of St Augustine: total poverty. We know little of his activities during the stormy years of the crusade, but, soon after, he resumed his "holy preaching." The new bishop of Toulouse, his personal friend, welcomed his aid and that of his disciples in this region, ravaged by the bands of Simon de Montfort, where Catholicism was being imposed by force on what remained of a decimated, harassed population, who accepted the change with sullen resentment. The small devoted group of Friars Preachers did its best to overcome this hostility and to effect a change of heart. When Dominic attended the Lateran Council, the Fathers, who were struggling to prevent the multiplication of sects, showed some reluctance to approving of a new congregation. However, Dominic had his way, though the Council instructed him to adopt one of the existing Rules, not to invent one of his own. His choice fell on the Rule he had imposed on the nuns at Prouille, that of the Augustinian canons. But when founding the Order of the Friars Preachers and its Rule he made some small yet signal changes in it.

The fundamental condition of the Dominican way of life was absolute poverty. Not, like that of Cîteaux, factitious; but the real poverty of Christ. The contemporary world had been corrupted by wealth and this was the first thing to attack. Chapter XXVI, entitled "Concerning the Rejection of Property," contains this vital precept: "We shall not accept in any manner either property or a fixed income." Thus in a social order in which land was ceasing to be the only form of wealth, a religious community was established which for the first time did not rely for its maintenance on real estate, which no longer lived on the produce of its own land, but on charity, begging its bread from door to door. The Dominican had no personal possessions, except books. But these were the tools of his trade; his mission was to preach the true doctrine and to combat manfully the demons of unbelief, cunning foes whom only the Light of the Spirit could lay low. Therefore he had to train himself, to develop his reasoning faculty, to read and study. And, as the masters of the schools had shown, studying involved teamwork. So the Dominicans, like the cathedral canons and Benedictine monks, lived a corporate life. Not like these latter to join in chanting hour by hour the praises of the Lord. For the Dominican the ritual was more flexible and simpler; he need not trouble over-much about fixed hours and could, whenever necessary, cut short his devotions. He was not subservient to the cosmic rhythms which for many centuries, in less disturbed ages, had set the tempo of devotion in the monasteries. For the vocation of the Friar Preacher necessitated his entering the lists whenever need arose; the enemy was at the gate. There was no coming to grips with him in solitude, in the desert or even in the fields. No, he must be confronted among men, in the heart of this new world where the countryside no longer held first place; in the towns. Hence the founding of Dominican monasteries in the great centers of population, where their message was most needed. But the Dominican House differed from the cloister since the friars were not secluded in it; it was no more than a rest-house to which, their labors ended, they came to share the food begged in the streets, and to sleep. But like the cathedral cloister the Dominican friary was a place of intellectual activity, indeed its chief function was educational. In each a friar read out passages from the Scriptures and commented on them, and one of the rules was that every Dominican should possess a copy, written in his own hand, of the Bible, also of Peter Lombard's *Sentences*, a compendium of the dicta of thirteenth-century theology, and the *History* of Peter Comestor (the "devourer" of books) which provided concrete themes for preaching. These books were neither bulky nor ornate like those from the monastic libraries used for the celebration of the Mass or for private meditation. They served as manuals ready to hand that the Friar Preacher kept in his wallet so as to verify a detail, if needed; for he had already memorized their substance. "They (the Friars) must not base their studies on the writings of pagans and philosophers—even if they consult them on occasion. Nor should they study the secular sciences or even the so-called liberal arts unless the Master of the Order or the Chapter General makes an exception in the case of certain persons.

The Superior can grant the students a dispensation provided it is of such a nature that their studies will not be interrupted, and they are not handicapped by questions relating to divine service or other such matters." These militants in the doctrinal arena had to be well equipped; so dispensations were frequently granted. For Dominic, we repeat, was a man of learning and the new Order took form at the heart of the scholastic disciplines of the period.

In all the great university towns—Montpellier, Bologna, Oxford and, above all, Paris—Dominican foundations came to take an ever greater part in theological research; indeed they soon became its seminal centers.

After stemming from a cathedral chapter, the Order of Preachers had broken away from it so as the better to adjust to contemporary needs the educational activities of the cathedral, to place them at the service of the Holy See and under its control. The Franciscan Order was composed of different elements; it stemmed from the urban laity and reflected its spiritual frustrations. St Francis, son of a well-to-do merchant, belonged to a commune which had elected a Cathar mayor. In his early days he had led a life of pleasure in the company of "young men about town," had composed love songs and joined in chivalrous exploits. Then he was caught up in the spiritual unrest that was affecting the middle class in the Southern towns. Not that he heard the call of Catharism; it was the voice of Christ he listened to. And when, like Peter Waldo, he stripped himself of his possessions, cast off his clothes and confronted his father, flinging at his feet his personal adornments, the bishop of Assisi covered his nakedness with his cloak. Francis stayed in the Church and he too was a mendicant. But he never ceased singing, he was "God's songster," and, like the troubadours, idolized a mistress, in his case Lady Poverty. He preached not only penitence, but the beauty of the universe, Brother Sun and all the stars. Some young men, friends of his, joined forces with him and, as Christ had done, he sent forth his disciples on the highways, empty-handed, clad in sackcloth. They lived among the poor, worked in the fields to earn their daily bread, and in the evenings these "jongleurs of God" gathered together to sing the perfect joy of poverty. If it so happened that they could not find work they could always beg their bread from door to door; God would not let them die of hunger.

In 1209 Innocent III, who looked with a friendly eye on the mendicant sects, gave his approval to the preaching of Francis and his very simple Rule, based on texts from the New Testament. The "Minors" (as Francis called them) started visiting the larger cities; the first of them reached Paris in 1219. To begin with they were looked askance at, suspected of being heretics, and required to produce their "visa" from the Pope. But by 1233 they had established themselves in all the towns of northern France. This was the time when the status of wives and daughters of the nobility was being ameliorated and women were beginning to form religious associations of their own. Born of a knightly family in Assisi, St Clara founded a community of nuns (the Poor Clares) modeled on the Minors of her friend Francis. And an Order of Tertiaries was formed consisting of women who, without completely breaking with the world, observed an apostolic rule of life appropriate to their condition. Francis, meanwhile, drew ever closer to a true fraternity with Jesus and even identified himself with Him so perfectly that "in the flame of his love" he received on his body "the Stigmata of the Crucified." Everywhere he was venerated as a saint, exemplar of a new perfection in keeping with the urge to poverty which now prevailed among the younger townsfolk: their will to strip themselves of worldly goods, to dispense charity, and to obey the precept of Francis that his followers should be constantly "rejoicing in the Lord," singing hymns of joy. He did not combat heresy with the sword but with the voice of reason and with the example of his life, a life of all-embracing kindness. He did more than any other to make the simple Gospel truths an actuality, to show that the Christian life was feasible. Next after Christ, St Francis is the dominant figure of Christian history and it is no exaggeration to say that what remains of true Christianity in the modern world derives directly from him.

He was not a priest and never dreamt of becoming one; nor did his disciples. But he showed no hostility towards the priests and in his addresses to the people aimed at aiding those whose daily task it was to celebrate the Mass. In its conflict with the Cathars and Waldensians the Church stressed the efficacy of the Eucharist and it was now that the dogma of Transubstantiation was promulgated by the Lateran Council. Representations of the Last Supper were carved on church portals in towns contaminated by heresy, at Beaucaire, Saint-Gilles and Modena, and Jesus was shown giving the morsel of bread even to his betrayer Judas. Thus St Francis labored in the defence of the priests. "If the Blessed Virgin is so greatly—and so rightly—venerated, since she bore Christ in her most holy womb; if the blessed Baptist trembled with awe and dared not touch the holy head of his Lord; if the tomb in which Christ's body lay for several days is treated with such respect, how saintly, righteous and worthy must that man be who takes Christ Jesus in his hand, holds Him to his heart, raises Him to his lips and gives Him as nourishment to others." And again, in his spiritual testament, St Francis wrote: "Even if I find poor priests leading a worldly life, I would not dare—even if I had the wisdom of Solomon—to preach against their wishes in the parishes where they dwell. For these priests too (like all other priests) I am bound to fear, to cherish, and to honor as my masters. So I have no wish to draw attention to their sins, since I discern in them the Son of God, and they are my superiors. The reason why I treat them thus is that in this world I find no perceptible token of that same Son of Almighty God other than His most holy body and most sacred blood, which these men consecrate and which they alone dispense to others. And I desire above all to honor and venerate these very holy mysteries and to situate them in places worthily adorned." A humble and reverent auxiliary of the priesthood, the Franciscan message began by being extremely simple, rather an example of a way of life than a logical exegesis—hence its remarkable success. The cardinals, however, desired to organize it, reinforce it, and the Holy See to give it a sound doctrinal foundation. Despite the efforts of St Francis and some of his disciples, the Order of the Minorites was gradually transformed into a militia of priests and intellectuals on the lines of the Preaching Friars. Established in monasteries, the Franciscans had to abandon their life of poetic vagrancy, their roamings in the gracious Umbrian countryside. They were given books and professors; studia were set up for them in Paris and other educational centers. From 1225 onward they constituted a second "army of knowledge" under the pope's control and, in heretically minded cities, were called on to participate in the clerical campaign of repression.

For Innocent III had decided that henceforth this campaign could be made most effective by a planned co-ordination of parishes in which the priests, aided by the mobile forces of the mendicant orders, would be able to exercise a strict surveillance over their flocks. Throughout Christendom there soon developed an elaborate network of parishes. In the rural districts of France the parochial system was brought into application in the thirteenth century and it became the custom to describe each peasant as a "parishioner" of such and such a place. He was not allowed to partake of the Sacrament elsewhere than in his parish church and attempts were made to regularize his devotions. The Lateran Council bade all laymen communicate and make confession once a year and the local priest was called on to track down those who sought to evade these duties, so as to detect clandestine heretics. Hence the humorous descriptions of " Prospère," village curé and petty tyrant, in the fabliaux, the *Roman de Renart* and the cycles of comic poems. In new districts of the larger towns similar parochial units were established, and the bishop was held personally responsible for this supervision of the mores of the population in all parts of his diocese.

The bishop had two well-defined functions. First of these was the repression of heresy. As a *judex ordinarius* he summarily heard complaints of breaches of ecclesiastical discipline. But there was also a special procedure: the inquisition. This involved preliminary inquiry, and the bishop took action without waiting for the formal laying of a complaint. Enacted by the Lateran Council, this special procedure was soon applied throughout southern France. Persons commonly reputed to be heretics were arrested and questioned in public; means were taken to expedite their confessions. If they persisted in their false beliefs they were made over to the secular authorities, to be burnt at the stake; otherwise the inquisitor imposed on them a penance, sometimes a pilgrimage, oftener the " wall " (i.e. life imprisonment). This repressive function was vested in the bishop. The duty of the priest was to rid his parish of evil-doers, to preserve the Christian community, already segregated from Jews and lepers, from any risk of being infected with the germs of heresy. The bishop kindled the faggots that burnt the heretics; but it was also his task to spread the light of Christian truth. This second mission, that of making known the dogmas of the Church and proclaiming the eternal verities, was traditional; as was that of teaching in person or, anyhow, promoting educational facilities in the city.

As a centralized monarchy, the Catholic Church entrusted directly to the pope the management of the great student centers, the academies of theology in which the tenets of the Church were precisely formulated. Henceforth they were a pivotal element of the machinery needed by a religion seeking to enroll the intelligentsia in its defence.

The chief educational centers were reorganized as more coherent units, the "universities," over which, though they were exempted from the bishops' control, the pope sought to exercise authority. Already for a long time teachers and students had been banding themselves together in guilds (like the trade guilds in the towns), with a view to freeing themselves from vexatious interference by the local authorities and the domination of the cathedral clique. In Paris the guild had wrested from the king and the chapter of Notre-Dame substantial freedoms. Innocent III took official notice and, when his legate drew up the statutes of this *universitas magistrum et scolarium parisientium*, this was to keep a stricter control of its activities and link it more closely to the Holy See. The doctrine of Amalric of Bena was proscribed and ten teachers who persisted in propagating it were burned at the stake. Books with "dangerous" tendencies were banned and in the university of Paris professors were forbidden to acquaint their pupils with Aristotle's *Metaphysics* and the commentaries of Avicenna. Finally, it was decided that the mendicant orders were most trustworthy and members of them were appointed to the senior professorships in theology. The disciplines of logic were the *sine qua non ;* no time was to be wasted on aesthetic problems or "vain researches." In the early thirteenth century the university of Paris became one vast "thinking machine" and in the faculty of arts, where theological students took their preliminary courses, dialectics reigned supreme. The "lesson" involving direct contact with an author gave place to organized debates in which young men learned to bandy arguments and to make an expert usage of the syllogism—in short to prepare themselves for the doctrinal disputations of their later years. Ceasing to serve as an approach to the study of literature, grammar became an exercise in practical linguistics and verbal logic; its chief function was to analyse modes of expression with an eye to the handling of language as a vehicle of close reasoning. What, then, was the point of reading Ovid or Virgil, of seeking to get pleasure out of literature, now that words were no more than the machine-tools of constructive argumentation, and dialectics the science of sciences? This way of thinking soon dried up the well-springs of humanism, and scholastic disquisition, stripped of all ornaments, tended more and more towards an arid formalism. Thus in Paris and at the other great universities, at Oxford and Toulouse, whose activities were mobilized to combat heresy, there rapidly developed a theological discipline of an unprecedented rigor and precision.

This theology was paramount in the evangelical preaching in the towns, where the Dominicans and Franciscans took the lead. Specialists in the field of verbal eloquence, they compelled the bishop and his priests to recognize their superior qualifications. Mixing as they did with the people on an equal footing, they were more alive to the stirrings of the new mentality, knew how to hold the interest of large crowds and to touch their hearts. They employed everyday language and homely metaphors, enlivening their discourses with anecdotes adapted to the social status of the audience they addressed. Nor did they fail to note the propaganda value of the miracle play; it was now that Parisians flocked to see the first of the *Miracles de Notre-Dame*. And art, too, was called on to serve, more perhaps than ever before, as an instrument of edification.

During the first half of the thirteenth century the mendicant orders did not, as yet, take any active part in artistic creation. They had hardly "settled down"; so far their monasteries were ramshackle edifices, their oratories mere sheds, and they left the task of adorning places of worship to the clergy. But they advised the ecclesiastical authorities to embellish their churches and provided them with iconographic themes culled from their sermons. Though he banned images from the Cistercian abbeys, St Bernard had agreed that figurative art could have a place in city churches "to enable the bishops who have charge of souls, both the wise and the ignorant, to stimulate by visible images the 'carnal' devotion of the people, when they find themselves unable to do this with spiritual images." St Francis, too, wished churches, sheltering as they did the body of our Lord, to be "finely decorated." Thus in the days of the first Dominican and Franciscan missions a new generation of cathedrals —enduring sermons in stone—arose above the cities and their growth was surprisingly rapid. Work on Notre-Dame of Paris was brought to a speedy close in 1250 (after nearly a century's delays). The rising prosperity of the middle class, a more efficient canalization of alms and the pressing need to instill instant conviction of the Christian verities led to more rapid building. The men who toiled in the cathedral workyards were fired by a holy zeal. Begun in 1191, the new cathedral of Chartres was completed twenty-six years later and work at Amiens progressed even more rapidly. At Reims, where the first stone was laid in 1212, all the essential parts of the cathedral had been erected by 1233. More money was expended on cathedral building, far more workers were employed, than on even the most ambitious secular enterprises of the age. The chapters now left the conduct of building operations to technicians who moved from place to place, wherever their services were required, and the notebooks of one of them, Villard de Honnecourt, have survived. They show that he had a keen interest in mechanical appliances such as cranes for lifting heavy weights, which ensured an economy of labor and speeded up completion of the work in hand. He also had a gift for the practical application of mathematical formulas and for envisaging schematically the overall effect of an edifice. For the architects—entitled *docteurs ès pierre*—had mastered the mathematics taught in the schools and indeed described themselves as "masters." None the less the edifices they were called on to design still embodied, in inert matter, the ideology of the professors and their dialectics. The cathedrals acted, in fact, as visual demonstrations of Catholic theology.

More than ever, this theology identified the essence of God with light. The better to combat the lures of Catharism, the best thinkers of the day reverted to the hierarchies propounded by the Pseudo-Areopagite, but sought to buttress them with more telling arguments, incorporating recent discoveries in the field of physics. Robert Grosseteste, who launched the new schools of Oxford, read Greek, was acquainted with the works of Ptolemy, with the new astronomy and the Arab commentaries on Aristotle's *De Caelo*. He, too, conceived of God as light and the whole material universe as a brilliant sphere radiating from a central nucleus into the three dimensions of Space. All human knowledge sprang from the spiritual effluence of this primal, uncreated light. Sin makes the body opaque; hence our inability to see directly the emanations of the Light Divine. But in the body of Christ, God and man, the spiritual universe and the material universe regained their pristine unity. Jesus and by the same token the cathedral, which was His symbol, were thus regarded as the center from which all proceeds and in which all things are clarified: the Trinity, the Word made Flesh, the Church, mankind, the whole created world. And these ideas pointed the way to a precise aesthetic. "Best of all things, most delectable, most beautiful is natural light; it is light that constitutes the perfection and beauty of all material forms." Grosseteste stated in philosophical terms what was obscurely sensed by the Franciscans in their *laudes* of St Clara. "Her angelic face was brighter and lovelier after prayer, such was the joy resplendent in it. Verily our generous and gracious Lord flooded with his rays his humble little spouse, so that she shed the divine light on everything around her." And the Dominican Albertus Magnus defined beauty as "a resplendence of form."

Thus even more than the edifices from which they originated the second generation of cathedrals were illuminated with the celestial light. The upper part of the Sainte-Chapelle in Paris is a vast net spread out to trap light in its meshes, and the walls vanish into thin air, so that the whole interior is flooded with a radiance more evenly distributed than ever before—which would certainly have delighted Suger. At Reims Jean d'Orbais constructed windows executed in open-work, whose designs Villard de Honnecourt copied in his notebook and which soon came into vogue everywhere. Master Gaucher suppressed all the tympana of the façade and replaced them with stained glass. Everywhere rose windows blossomed forth, sometimes expanding so as to touch the masonry of the buttresses. Forming perfect circles, symbols of the rotation of the cosmos, they also signified the cyclic flux and reflux of light inaugurated by the Creator on the First Day.

Grosseteste's views were set forth in detail in his treatise *De physicis, lineis, angulis et figuris*, and were based on strictly applied geometry. From them derived the luminous precision of thirteenth-century architecture, its clarity and its logic, rigorous as a syllogism. It reflected the approach to knowledge promoted by the Faculty of Arts. Thus the new cathedral gives an impression of being less eloquent than its predecessors; it caters less for the pleasure of the eye, is more concerned with the rational disposition of its parts and aims at perfect cogency, like the proof of a scholastic theorem. For its forms were inspired by schoolmen who, year in, year out, furbished the arms of their intelligence in order to hold their own in the great jousts of Eastertide, public debates in which they nimbly plied the rapiers of their wit. Like them the master-of-works proceeded dialectically, sorting out homologous parts, then the parts of those parts, before reassembling them in a logical catena. Soaring heavenwards in a geometrical progression woven in strands of light, the cathedral owed much of its compelling power to the intelligence of the master mind behind it.

Its adornments were not selected for their charm; their purpose was to give the assembled congregation a visual corroboration of the Faith, a résumé of Christian *sapientia* and an antidote to heresy. Above all to inculcate a theology of the kind approved of by the Church. Intended to appeal directly to the masses, the images were placed well in view. At Reims and Amiens the statues quitted niches and recesses and advanced towards the congregation, silent sponsors of the efficacy of the ritual. Their message was a reminder of the sacred function of the prelacy, of the masters teaching in the schools, of priests who consecrated the bread and wine, of bishop and inquisitor. Melchizedek is shown presenting the Host to Saul accoutred like a medieval knight. In his attacks on the Waldensian heresy the sculptor did not represent Christ as poor, betrayed, alone, but as the founder of a church, escorted like a bishop by his clergy. Since the Cathars denied the Incarnation, the Redemption and even the Creation, the figurations in the cathedrals proclaimed with no uncertain voice the omnipotence of the Triune God: Creator, Incarnate, Redeemer.

THE BRONZE DOORS

A whole community of metal-workers lived in the Austrasian forests and the best weapons in the early medieval world had come from their smithies. It was largely thanks to these that the Franks had succeeded in bringing all the western continent under their sway. When their conquests had reinstated the Roman Empire, and Charlemagne, a new Augustus, was moved to erect monuments like those of the Caesars in his ancestral domain, he gave orders for ancient bronzes to be brought from Rome to Aix-la-Chapelle. Henceforward the craft of bronze-working played a leading part in the new imperial art. Suger, too, when he sought to revive the Carolingian tradition in his reconstruction of the royal abbey of Saint-Denis, which housed the tombs of the kings of France, decided to provide it with bronze doors. But the wide diffusion of this type of ornament in twelfth-century Europe testifies above all to the prestige of the Germanic Empire in the great days of Frederick Barbarossa.

The Slav kingdoms of the East acknowledged his suzerainty. When around 1155 the Bishop of Plock planned to embellish his church he commissioned historiated bronze panels from Saxony (or Lorraine) to decorate the entrance. Unfortunately for him these were stolen en route; they are now in the cathedral of St Sophia in Old Novgorod. This was then a flourishing market town where enterprising German traders bartered cloth for honey, wax and Russian furs. These panels depict, in a somewhat uncouth way, scenes from Holy Writ, and give them the barbarian accent of the paintings in the Rhenish Bibles. The doors of the cathedral at Gniezno, however, are thoroughly classical in spirit. They narrate in the style of the Saxon renascence episodes in the life of St Adalbert, friend of the Emperor Otto III, who shortly before the year 1000 preached the Gospel in Bohemia, died a martyr's death at the hands of the Prussians, and whose remains were preserved in Gniezno, the Polish capital.

During the same period the Empire consolidated its hold on Tuscany and southern Italy, on the old Lombard duchies and on the kingdom of Sicily, the heiress to which married Barbarossa's son. In 1180 at Pisa the bronzesmith Bonannus made figures of angels and shepherds for the entrance of the Grotto of the Nativity; the classicizing influence of the Hildesheim bronzes can be seen in these figures and they have nothing of the barbaric violence of those on the door of San Zeno at Verona. Fifteen years later at Benevento and Monreale other bronzes set the imperial seal, at once Germanic and Roman, of the Hohenstaufens on churches otherwise decorated wholly in the Byzantine style.

BONANNUS OF PISA (DIED ABOUT 1183). BRONZE DOOR (PORTA DI SAN RANIERI) OF PISA CATHEDRAL, 1180

BRONZE DOOR WITH SCENES FROM THE LIFE OF ST ADALBERT, ABOUT 1175. CATHEDRAL OF GNIEZNO (POLAND).

109

BRONZE DOOR OF BENEVENTO CATHEDRAL, DETAIL. LATE 12TH CENTURY.

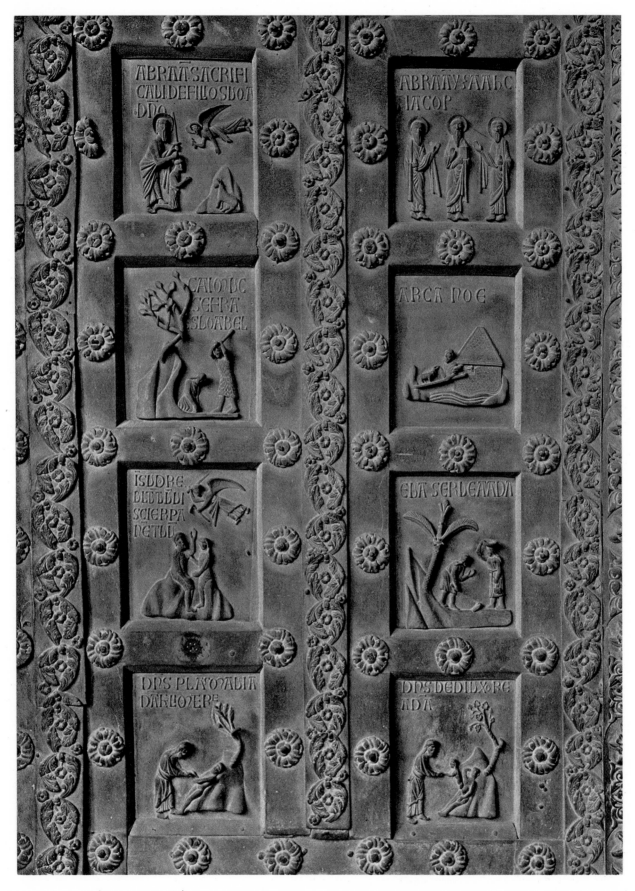

BONANNUS OF PISA (DIED ABOUT 1183). BRONZE DOOR OF THE MAIN ENTRANCE OF MONREALE CATHEDRAL, DETAIL. FINISHED IN 1186.

ANTIHERETICAL ART

The spate of heresies in southern Christendom, the alarming progress of Catharism and of a host of obscure sects which denied the primacy of Rome made the proclamation of the truth, that is to say of Catholic dogma, a matter of extreme urgency. For the enlightenment of the masses, whom the "Perfects" were discouraging with growing success from attending services conducted in it, the church, it was felt, should body forth on its façade, for all to see, a sermon in stone, easy to grasp and carrying conviction. The sculpture in the portal should no longer have as its leitmotiv a vision of the Last Day, but convey in the simplest possible terms its message that in Jesus God was made man, recount His life on earth and demonstrate the efficacy of His sacrifice.

On the façade of the Ripoll monastery scenes from the lives of Moses, David and Solomon had been displayed in successive, super-imposed tiers, as in liturgical manuscripts. In 1160-1170, however, in the heart of the region most affected by the Cathar schism, the portals of Saint-Gilles were crowded with dramatic antiheretical figurations. We see the apostles, witnesses to the Word incarnate, stalwart athletes of the True Faith, standing between the columns of an ancient temple, vigorously trampling underfoot the powers of evil and the sophistries of the schismatics. The frieze above illustrates the Gospel narrative, culminating on the lintel of the largest portal in a representa-tion of the Last Supper. It affirms the verity of the Eucharist, the sacrament whereby Jesus remains a living presence in this world until His triumphal return at the Last Judgment.

The theme of the Last Supper was also treated in the cathedral of Modena by contemporary artists very close to Benedetto Antelami. At Parma, for the decoration of the ambo of the cathedral, the Gospel pulpit, Antelami was persuaded by the local theologians to revert to the Byzantine image of the Deposition from the Cross. This representation of the dead Christ on Calvary, flanked by soldiers and the Holy Women (Mary is kissing His right hand), made it clear to every beholder that God was not only spirit and light, but took flesh to suffer and to die so as to bring redemption to mankind. But the same artist also had a gift for expressing the joyful side of God's creation. On the front of the church he placed illustrations of an allegorical Carolingian poem ascribed to Alcuin recounting the combat of Winter and Spring. Here Spring, Symbol of the triumph of life, of nature's resurrection and also that of Jesus and all mankind, is given the form of a chaste and simple maiden of high degree. To this simplicity is due the singular grace and winsomeness of the young body.

PORCH OF THE ABBEY CHURCH OF SANTA MARIA AT RIPOLL (CATALONIA). MID-12TH CENTURY.

114

SAINT-GILLES DU GARD. ABOUT 1160-1170.

KING DAVID, DETAIL OF THE FAÇADE OF THE CATHEDRAL OF FIDENZA (BORGO SAN DONNINO).
1214-1218. (SCULPTURES ATTRIBUTED TO BENEDETTO ANTELAMI)

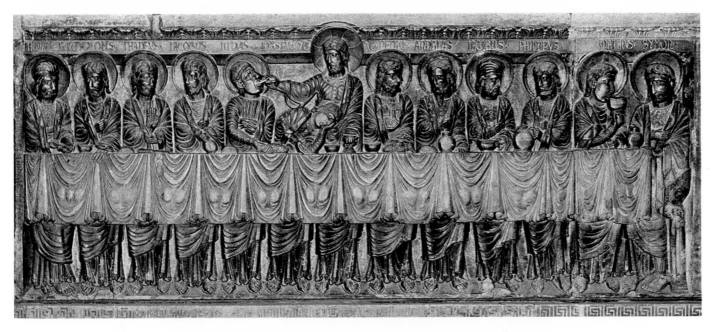

ANSELMO DA CAMPIONE AND HIS WORKSHOP. THE LAST SUPPER, 1160-1175.
DETAIL OF THE CHOIR SCREEN IN MODENA CATHEDRAL.

BENEDETTO ANTELAMI (ABOUT 1150-ABOUT 1230). THE DESCENT FROM THE CROSS, 1178. MARBLE.
PARMA CATHEDRAL.

117

THE BAPTISTERY OF PARMA WITH THE NORTH PORTAL (PORTAL OF THE VIRGIN) BY BENEDETTO ANTELAMI. 1196-1200.

118

3

THE PORCH

"O Thou who hast said 'I am the door, by me if any man enter in, he shall be saved,' show us clearly of what dwelling-place Thou art the door, and who they are to whom, and at what hour, Thou wilt open it... Surely the house of which Thou art the door is the heaven in which thy Father dwells." The French cathedral was a visible, abiding answer to this prayer of the Cistercian William of Saint-Thierry. Jesus is the Way, and the cathedral, body of Christ, has portals opening in many directions. The function of its transept is to provide, on the north and south of the building, porches as spacious and impressive as the one facing west. These entrances gradually developed into complex, almost independent units. The beholder's gaze, intercepted by masses of houses huddling round the edifice which, owing to the absence of broad avenues, cannot be viewed in proper perspective, is limited, as he approaches, to the upper parts of the building. With its portals the cathedral extends a welcome to the townsfolk, on all sides, and their mission is to instruct, to serve in short as schools. Schools that were less cut off from the world than those of the cloisters or the booths where crowds of students sat at the feet of learned pedagogues. The portals did not talk Latin but a language that everyone was, or should be, capable of understanding. Their function was to popularize the teaching of the doctors and this was held to justify the lavish expenditure of money and materials, of art and labor, which absorbed so large a part of the alms and taxes levied on all sides, the huge sums exacted by the bishop and his canons from merchants in the town and the peasants of the nearby countryside. In its porches the cathedral demonstrated its pastoral vocation—of propagating that true faith which had been clarified and consolidated by the schoolmen working in the centers of learning attached to it.

The front parts of the churches which preceded the cathedrals had been used for funerary rites. Thus, they had given prominence to representations of the Last Judgment and visions of man's lot after death, in which the beholder found intimations of a world beyond the grave, beyond Space and Time, and of a glorious hereafter bathed in the white radiance of eternity. The scene of the Last Day still held a prominent place in the cathedral porch, but it was differently arranged and carried new significances. The figure of Christ in Judgment towers above the Portico de la Gloria carved by Master Mateo in 1188 for the cathedral of Santiago de Compostela, but here there is little or nothing of the ethereal transcendency of the Christs of the Second Coming in Cluniac Aquitaine. He has the body of a living man. Yet this Jesus, escorted by angels, has not yet come down to the level of the people; He has, rather, the aspect of a priest celebrating the divine liturgy, or a king who has set forth around him—as at a coronation ceremony—all the richest objects in his treasure. Here they are relics of the Passion, preserved in fine linen, and attendant angels display them to the worshippers, as being the earthly weapons of the divine victory over death, instruments of the salvation of mankind.

The Compostela portal contains many statues and reliefs. But in royal France the cathedral porches sheltered a far greater number of the participants in the divine tragedy. Grouped together, they compose a didactic and dramatic exposition, in visual terms, of the tenets of Catholic dogma. For some time past all the devices of stage performances had been used for making clear to the populace the purport of the liturgic rites, and these "mystery plays" were given static form in sculpture. In those that took place at Christmas actors recited to the audience passages from the Scriptures foretelling the Incarnation, and played the parts of Isaiah, Jeremiah, Moses, David. From these performances derived the statues of prophets, of Simeon, Elizabeth, John the Baptist, the angel Gabriel and all the Biblical characters held to be forerunners or prefigurations of Christ: Adam (first parent in the flesh of the Son of Man), the shepherd Abel, Noah, Melchizedek who "brought forth bread and wine"—paradigm of the Last Supper. So as to make them more convincing the churchmen who drew up the iconographic programs ceased to embody the sacred figures in the architecture; they stepped forth from the wall towards the public. The tympanum was heightened so that the scenes displayed on it could be given wide dimensions and deployed on successive tiers for all to see. The number of free-standing figures increased. In the numerous portals of Chartres the thematic material of the statuary covers an immense field, including not only the entire Old and New Testaments, but also the Creation and all the holy intercessors whose relics were preserved in the Cathedral, with their respective virtues represented for the edification of the sinner.

Jean Le Loup had made plans for an enormous portal in the façade of Reims; the Archbishop, Henri de Braisne, wanted it to be even more grandiose than that of Amiens, whose see was suffragan to his. Work on it was completed by Maître Gaucher, who replaced the tympanum with stained-glass windows and transferred to the gable the scenes which figured on it. Most of the statues had been carved under the supervision of Le Loup. When between 1244 and 1252, Gaucher installed them he rearranged them so as to conform to the new trend of theological thought, in which the cult of the Virgin was taking an ever larger place. It had been intended to place the patron saints of the cathedral—St Nicasius, St Remigius and Pope Celestine—in the center; now they were relegated to the left side-portal on whose arches are scenes of the Passion and the Resurrection. That on the right, devoted to the Last Judgment, housed the figurations of the prophets, while the central portal was occupied in its entirety by the Virgin. None of the statues made in the Reims workyards has the beauty and emotive fervor of the Amiens Visitation and Presentation in the Temple.

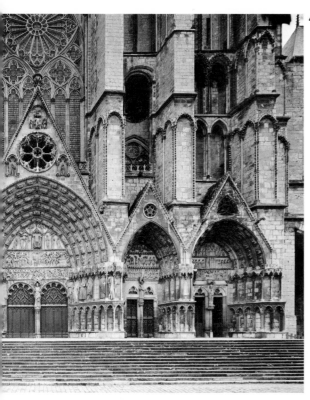

125

THE CREATION

At the beginning of the century Amalric's heresy had been ruthlessly exterminated; it was clearly necessary for the Christian not to confuse God with his creatures and a clear-cut distinction between the specific values of body, soul and spirit had to be made. Not that matter was to be condemned *per se* as alien to God and pitted against him as a rival, adverse principle; indeed this Manichaean dualism was the greatest peril of the age. Cautiously interpreted, the theology of Dionysius provided a satisfactory solution. For it represented nature as issuing from God and returning to Him, absorbed in His oneness. This flux and reflux was the work of love; God's creatures were envisaged as substances distinct from the godhead which existed independently of them, but conforming in a fashion, like a Platonic "idea," to a divine exemplar. Yet though illumined, filled with Him, they are but reflections of the divine light. According to Dionysius and the orthodox theology inspired by him, all material things participate in God's splendor, celebrate Him, and enable us to know Him.

This was how that joyous optimist Francis of Assisi saw the world of matter. "How describe the emotions that came over him when he found in each created thing the signature of the Creator and tokens of his power and loving-kindness. Even as the Three Holy Children in the fiery furnace bade all the elements praise and glorify the Creator of the universe, so Francis, filled with the spirit of God, found in all the elements, all creatures, good grounds for praising, glorifying, blessing the Maker of the world. When his gaze fell on a meadow gay with flowers he made haste to preach to them, as though they had the gift of reason, and called on them to praise the Lord. Wheatfields and vineyards, flowing streams, verdant gardens, earth and fire, the air and the winds—all these he exhorted, with entire sincerity and simplicity, to love God and gladly to obey Him. He called all created things his brothers and by a gift peculiar to himself could read their inmost secrets, as though already, freed of this mortal coil, he were living in the glorious freedom of the children of God." Brother of Jesus, Francis also felt himself a brother of the sun, wind, birds of the heavens—and of death. As he roved the Umbrian countryside, all its beauties kept him company in a jubilant cortège. This glad communion with all things great and small accorded with the carefree *joie de vivre* of the youth of the feudal courts, and helped to lead back to God the bands of boys and girls who danced around the maypoles. For it was by making much of nature, the wild life of field and forest, the soft sweet air of summer dawns, the bloom of ripening grapes, that the Church of the cathedral builders had the best chance of recalling to the fold the sportive knights, the troubadours and the peasantry still half convinced of the powers of the old nature-gods. St Bernard had said the same thing with his usual bluntness. "You shall see for yourselves that one can get honey from stones, oil from the hardest rocks."

By rehabilitating matter the Catholic theologians struck at the very root of Catharism and it may well be that the Franciscan canticles in praise of all God's creatures did most to vanquish heresy. By stressing the fact that the material universe was God's creation the theologians encouraged the cathedral builders to give a central place to images of the reconciliation of the visible world with the divine. The rose window in the north transept of Reims and the arches of Chartres show God creating light and the heavenly bodies, separating day from night, land from water, molding plants and animals and, lastly, man. They give in fact an imaged résumé of the Creation. Here, moreover, the narrative is not treated symbolically. In his commentary on the Book of Genesis, Thierry of Chartres had sought to harmonize Scripture with the physical science taught in the schools, and it now was possible to represent the incidents of the Creation clearly and realistically. In giving man his senses God had invited him to contemplate and study all his works as they really are—not to evoke them in a sort of waking dream. "The soul," Thomas Aquinas said, "has to get all its knowledge from the perceptible." It is by opening our eyes that we see these forms of God. Hence the tendency of the new school of thinkers to discard the fables, bestiaries, all the bric-à-brac of a more credulous age. Now that traders and missionaries were discovering lands hitherto veiled in mystery, real animals were taking the place of the fabulous monsters which knights errant used to encounter on their quests, and plants and trees seen every day in nearby forests replacing the symbolic flora of the Romanesque illuminators.

In the provinces where the new French art was born we find at the end of the twelfth century a keener interest in the factual; thus the famous *Roman de Renart* cycle has much to say of the avarice of the middle class, the boastfulness of braggart knights. Thomas de Cantimpré's *Book of Nature*, though still professing to give an allegorical interpretation of the phenomenal world, does not insist merely on the links between created beings and the "virtues," moral abstractions, it also dwells on their practical uses in the scheme of things. And, following Aristotle's example, all the theological treatises combine physics with their metaphysics, basing the latter no longer on analogies but on the evidence of the senses. For these epitomes of existing knowledge set out to be scientific; their compilers utilize data furnished by Greek and Arab experts. Optics, seconded by geometry, was given pride of place in these researches. This was, in Europe, the great age of astronomy and it was now that the first attempts were made to determine the exact measurements of the celestial bodies. It was also an age of naturalists. On his arrival in Paris in 1240 Albertus Magnus promptly acquainted his pupils, despite the ban on it, with Aristotle's *Physics*. "In matters of faith and morality," he said, "we must follow St Augustine rather than the philosophers, when they disagree. But when dealing with medicine I take my stand on Galen and Hippocrates, and when dealing with the nature of things I turn to Aristotle or some other expert on the subject." Albertus wrote a lengthy treatise *De Animalibus* in which he analysed in detail the characteristics of the fauna of Germany, where he had lived as a young man. For, like many of their contemporaries, the Dominicans sought relaxation in wild nature and even the towns were not so large or shut-in as to exclude the scents of spring; space

was found for gardens, vineyards, even wheatfields, within their new walls. The material civilization of thirteenth-century man, if still backward, did not cut him off from the outside world. He was still an open-air creature, the tempo and savor of whose life were bound up with the rhythms of nature and the seasons. Even the intellectuals spent more of their time in orchards and meadows than in their rooms, and all the cloisters were built around gardens full of flowers and birds. This intimacy with nature, this feeling that, far from being sinful, it bore the mark of God and revealed his visage, furnished the sap of the vegetation that twined its way around the pillars of Notre-Dame, fanning out in the capitals into a crown of leafage. Here the choir—completed around 1170—was still an intellectual construct, the lines and curves determined by a geometrical schema. But only ten years later, in the first bays of the nave, we find the flowers in the corbels taking less abstract forms, there is less symmetry, more of the diversity of nature, and it is becoming possible to identify each leaf, to distinguish every species. All the same these plants are still essentially signs; life, real life, begins to stir in them only in those parts of the building which were decorated after 1220.

But limits were set to the progress towards realism. Men were being encouraged to investigate the universe, but this was chiefly with a view to defining "types" more clearly and determining the role assigned to them by the Creator. For according to the Scholastics each individual, *qua* individual, belonged to a species whose type form is immanent *ante rem* in the mind of God. The task of the artist adorning the cathedral was to body forth that specific form, not its individual "accidents." He must therefore sort out the visual data and bring his reasoning faculty to bear on them. For God's mind, like man's, proceeds logically and the forms it engenders are precise as rays of light, that is to say geometrically ordered. When Villard de Honnecourt in his sketchbook constructs schematic figures of animals and of men wrestling or casting dice, the figures are built up with triangles, squares and curves, like the architecture of the cathedral as a whole. This rationalizing treatment brings out the underlying form, stripped of accidentals, which for the theologian is the true reality of the individual. Gothic imagery is accordingly subjected, perhaps even more strictly than Romanesque, to geometrical disciplines. The novelty here is that this geometry is applied not to products of the imagination but to objects actually perceived, and that their proportions are respected.

Moreover, these images, if isolated from each other, would have been meaningless. It was, then, the duty of the master-of-works so to arrange them that together, each in its due place, they combined to figure forth the created universe in its entirety. For all nature is one, like the God from whom its emanates, and the cathedral represents it as an organic whole. That is why its decorations are not mere samples or fragments, but a complete inventory, a "summa of creatures." Alan of Lille saw in nature the "vicegerent of Almighty God," a multiple reflection of His Oneness. This implies an affinity of all the parts of creation; harmonies and correspondences between them. The realism aimed at by French medieval art was a realism of essences; not of individuals but of a totality. Logical through and through, this art keeps to the hierarchies defined by Dionysius. It assigns to its due place each heavenly body, each species of the vegetable or animal kingdom, each order of existence; co-ordinates a multiplicity. For, as St Thomas Aquinas put it, "the divine nature keeps all things in their proper order, without confusion, in such a manner that all are linked together in a concrete coherence, each retaining its specific purity, even when involved in reciprocal co-ordinations." Here every word *tells*, and in this typically scholastic formulation we have a key to the Gothic aesthetic. In his *Paradiso* (I, 103-113) Dante expresses and expands the same idea.

> . . . All things whate'er they be
> Have order among themselves, this order being
> [the form
> That makes the universe resemble God.
> Here do the higher creatures see the impress
> Of the Eternal Power which is the end
> Whereto is made the Law set forth above.
> In the order that I speak of are inclined
> All natures by their destinies diverse
> More or less near towards their origins;
> Thus they move towards different ports
> O'er the great sea of being.

Lastly, the artist is told to represent the image of each being in its totality. "When a man subtracts anything from the perfection of a creature, it is from the perfection of God Himself that he subtracts it" (St Thomas Aquinas). All the laws of nature tend to that perfection. But they have to struggle to attain it and it is man's duty to eliminate all that obstructs the free play of nature's rhythms; this indeed is why God has endowed him with reason. Gothic man like Romanesque man was located at the center of the cosmos, linked to it by "reciprocal co-ordinations," and his body was subjected to its influences. His course of life was oriented by the courses of the stars, his "humors" were constantly affected by the elements. But, unlike Romanesque man, he was not overwhelmed by the scheme of things, nor its passive slave. By making him the highest of created beings, setting him at the apex of the hierarchies of the visible world, the Supreme Artist invited him to collaborate in His work. When creating him, He saw in man not merely a product but an agent of the creative process. That urge which lay behind the conversion of waste lands into tillage and vineyards, and the steady encroachment of towns on the countryside; that made the merchants flock to fairs, the knights go forth to battle, the Franciscans conquer souls—all the stirrings of the new spirit of the age were incorporated in the theology and the art of the cathedrals. Creation was still in progress and man called on to join in it with his works. Thus, along with the material world, labor of the hand was rehabilitated. Schoolmen at Paris and Oxford declaimed against the disdain for manual tasks which had prevailed among the aristocracy in periods of stagnation and had survived in Cluniac foundations. And while the Cathar "Perfecti" refused to stir a finger in the service of base matter, Cistercian monks, Premonstratensian canons, the Humiliati of Lombardy and the Little Brothers of St Francis all worked with their hands. They contributed thereby, so far as in them lay, to the continuous creation of the universe—like the humble peasants who at this same time were diverting streams to irrigate their crops and replacing tracts of brushwood with symmetrically ploughed fields. In the new manuals for the use of father confessors every profession based on honest toil was approved of and moralists sought out reasons to justify the profits accruing to it. The images of manual labors which figured in the portals of city churches reflected the rising prosperity of the working class, and when the members of a trade guild presented a stained-glass window to the cathedral they saw to it that the techniques of their craft were accurately represented. The triumph of the all-conquering worker was celebrated even in the House of God.

Central to this creative activity and the iconography of the cathedrals was the effigy of man. And Gothic man was of a new type. He had neither the emaciated face of the ascetic nor the rather bloated features of the prelate (apt to suffer from stone and to die of apoplexy). He bore no mark of the ravages of age or self-indulgence. An emanation of godhead, he is born in the prime of life, at that precise moment when his growth reaches its culminant point without the least hint as yet of the declining years. He might be twin brother of the potter-God we see at Chartres molding man in clay. To make his body misshapen for "realistic" ends or, like the Romanesque sculptors, distort it to fit into a specific setting would have involved "subtracting something" from God's perfection—sacrilege. The rational concordances between man and the cosmos should be perceptible in his effigy, since they determine his configuration. The bodies and faces of Adam and Eve at Bamberg conform to a perfectly constructed paradigm. They are among the Saved, entitled to a "glorious resurrection," washed clean of the taint of sin, the stigma of mortality. Already God's rays are falling on them, drawing them up towards the joys of heaven, and their faces are already lit with the happy smile of the angels.

But Gothic man is also a human individual. At Reims—among the saints and apostles, near the Virgin and Jesus (who is like him)—we see in her humility the maidservant of the Presentation. She is free, responsible for her acts, endowed with self-awareness. For the thirteenth-century Christian, who was learning to confess his sins each year, to look into himself and to trace the intentions behind his lapses, practised the introspection Abelard had counseled in the previous century. The figures which by order of the Doctors of the Church were set up on the fronts of churches were no longer mere symbols, but effigies of adult men and women, not puppets of blind forces but self-controlled, responsible beings. They are filled with that love which, aided by the faculty of reason, gives access to God's world of light. This is why their lips are quivering and their gaze seems held by a vision of enthralling splendor. For through the eyes the Light Divine strikes down to the secret places of the heart and kindles the flame of charity. The gaze, indeed, bulked large in the "light metaphysics" of the medieval theologians and did much to shape the destiny of Gothic man. True, this creature was born, will die, has sinned, lives in a space of time meted out by the courses of the stars. But now the great scholastics showed him that he could break the thrall of circumstance, free himself from the mutability of the sublunary world, shield himself against the powers of corruption and, participating in the moving immobility of celestial time, attune himself, even in earthly life, to his eternal archetype. Like Jesus who, though enfleshed as a time-bound man, none the less was before Abraham was, and lives and reigns throughout eternity.

4

TIME

The savants of the cathedral schools did not visualize God the Creator as "the Most High," a mysterious being, an Idea too transcendent for human minds to comprehend. According to them the universe was created *in principio*, i.e. *in verbo*, by the Word, the Son, incarnate throughout eternity. Thus the God who, in the bends of the Chartres arches, shapes Adam's body with his hand is so much like his creature that he might be Adam's brother. It is, in fact, a man, Jesus, who is making man in his image and imposing his features on all living beings. "Every created thing," Honorius of Autun affirmed, "is a shadow of the Truth and the Life"—in other words, of Christ. Since Christ existed at the first day and was, in his human *esse*, maker of all things, the world which his thought evoked from nothingness was given dimensions on the human scale.

The movement of the celestial spheres, in which we discern the underlying rhythms of the cosmos, is rotatory, and determines the cycle of days and nights and seasons. As the hours pass, the light of the sun moves from bay to bay of the Cistercian cloister, summoning to life its austere volumes and, similarly, the sequences of the liturgy, the choral chants joining in prayer the voices of the community, move in fixed cycles which, completed every day and every year in an eternal recurrence, form closed circles. However, this cyclic movement is much less frequent in the Gothic cathedral than in the Romanesque church. The Gothic mind preferred the straight line, vector of the historical process whose trend the thirteenth-century churchmen were beginning to perceive more clearly, the long straight path taken by the Christian and indeed all life on its way towards eternity. Straight, too, is the ray of light that represents the act of creation and divine grace, the line followed by the reasoning mind in action, by scholastic inquiry and all the intellectual progress of the age. Each proceeds unswervingly towards its terminal point. Only the rose window, symbol of fulfilled creation, in which God's light, issuing from its transcendent source, then converging back towards it, conforms, like the heavenly bodies, to the pattern of a closed circle.

The façade of the cathedral, embodiment in stone of God's omnipotence, figures forth another image of Time. Actually all that the sculptors responsible for it did was to revert to the symbols used in the calendars of Carolingian Gospel books. Figurations of the labors in the fields, coupled with the appropriate signs of the zodiac, they stand for the months of the year. Whereas the occupations of urban workers and even those of the merchants (though these latter were to some extent dependent on the seasons, since the great fairs took place at fixed times of the year) were relatively unaffected by the cosmic rhythms, the peasant observed them faithfully, they governed his way of life. In thirteenth-century Europe the towns, focal centers of all forms of artistic activity, opened widely on the countryside, and the lowlands around them contributed to the wealth of their inhabitants. The townsman usually owned some fields, cultivated a vineyard and kept sheep in sheds beside his house. The prosperity of the lords depended on the success of the crops and the cycle of the customary dues which formed the staple of their income was tied up with the cycle of field labors. Owners of large domains which were the source of their wealth, prelates and canons were far from being recluses; they conferred with their estate agents, marked out the tracts which were next to be cleared for cultivation and chose the sites of new villages. They made periodical visits to their country houses, kept track of the work being done, and at harvest time supervised the gathering of the crops and their storage in the tithe-barns, anxiously scanning the sky for threats of storms which might ruin the vine harvest. There was a feeling among these dignitaries of the Church that their quest of God and their interrogations of the heavenly bodies had an intimate connection with the daily round of agriculture. They contemplated Time, in fact, with a farmer's eye. For these men remained strangely backward by modern standards. Their homes were ill-lit, badly heated and even kings and bishops spent most of their time in the open, in woods, orchards, cloistered gardens. Everyone promptly took notice of the lengthening or shortening of the days, the first frost of the year, the timid awakening of Nature in the month when vines are pruned, and her seeming lethargy at the time of ploughing and that of sowing the early wheat. And all of them pictured the brazen fervor of high summer, the climbing of the sun towards the zenith, in a quite concrete guise: that of a drouthy harvester.

In the early twelfth century Romanesque sculptors had inscribed the sequence of the labors of the months in a half circle around the tympana. They were now set out by the French sculptors in long rows. Successive figures symbolizing the course of nature's time were enclosed in medallions isolating them from the plane surface of the wall. Italy transformed them into statues. In Venice, however, in St Mark's, the Months, arranged in low relief on vertical bands, recall the French iconography. But in the Romagna, at Parma and Modena, in the region where Rome was by way of regaining her true visage and ancient monuments were encouraging sculptors to disengage from the wall the effigies of grape-harvesters, wine-pressers and the cask-makers of the month of August, they took to producing stalwart, free-standing figurines like the bronze effigies of the dark powers of Earth revered by their remote forefathers.

Yet in Italy as in France, the month of May, "dead season" of agriculture, was represented as a horseman. His triumphal progress through the fields is a survival of the rites celebrating nature's rebirth in spring, but he also expresses the joy of the young knight riding forth, once winter's grip was ended, on some heroic foray. At Parma, however, in the heart of the fertile province of Emilia, the horseman brandishes a rustic implement, a bill-hook, used in this season for pruning trees and hedgerows.

TIME

1. Amiens Cathedral: the Labors of the Months and the Signs of the Zodiac. Frieze on the west front, details. Second quarter of the 13th century.

2. Notre-Dame, Paris: July, the Harvest. Sculpture on the door-jamb of the Portail de la Vierge. 12th century.

3. St Mark's, Venice: the Labors of the Months, detail. Bas-relief of the central doorway. 13th century.

4. Santa Maria della Pieve, Arezzo: sculptures on the vaulting of the central doorway. 12th-13th century.

5. Master of the Months of Ferrara (early 13th century). The months of April, July, September and December. Sculptures from the cathedral. Museo dell'Opera del Duomo, Ferrara.

6. Workshop of Benedetto Antelami. The Knight of May. 1206-1211. Baptistery of Parma.

7. Benedetto Antelami (c. 1150-c. 1230). Spring, about 1180. Baptistery of Parma (originally in the cathedral).

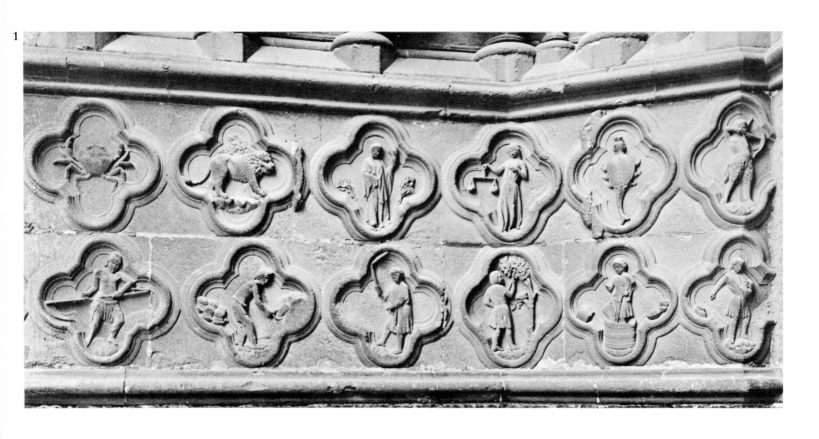

134

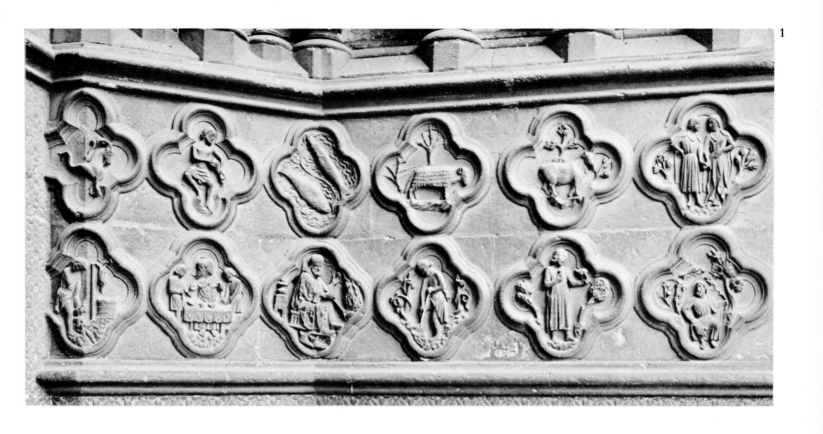

THE INCARNATION

Time plays no part in the recurrent ebb and flow which according to the mystical theology of Dionysius the Pseudo-Areopagite pervades the created universe: a movement oriented by two opposite polarities: God's loving-kindness and the love His creatures give Him in return. According to St Thomas Aquinas God's wisdom and goodness emanate from all His creatures, "but this process may also be regarded as a means of returning to the Supreme End, a return enabled by the gifts which alone unite us with that Supreme End, that is God, these gifts being sanctifying grace and our sense of the divine glory. In this emanation of creatures, which proceeds from their first principle, there is as it were a circulation or a respiration, inasmuch as all created beings tend to return to that from which they proceed, their primal essence. And in so doing they obey certain laws, governing alike their return and their procession." While basing his dialectic on Aristotle, St Thomas bore in mind the mystical doctrine of Dionysius. In the mid-thirteenth century the Dominican and Franciscan masters lecturing in the Paris schools at once achieved lucidity and reconciled the rationalism of Aristotelian thought with St Bernard's appeal to the emotions. Using logical methods, they sought to discover the laws of that creative "respiration," like the act of breathing, of which Aquinas speaks and at discovering the God of the natural world, identical with the God of the supernatural. But their *primum mobile* was love, the love that Dante speaks of in his *Purgatorio*.

> As fire moves, rising to the zenith
> By reason of its very form, made to ascend
> To the place where it lasts best in its substance,
> Even so the living soul is filled with yearning,
> A movement of the spirit, and never rests
> Until it has enjoyed the object of its love.

For at the point of junction between love and reason, at the precise point where the forth-flowing divine light encounters the returning tide, where nature and supernature, time and eternity meet, is Christ, God made man, "light born of light," yet clad in human flesh. From its earliest phase at Saint-Denis on, Gothic art strove to express the Incarnation and elaborated the imagery seen to perfection in the thirteenth-century cathedrals. Inspired directly by the Gospels, it was imbued with the spirit of the underground movements which already in the eleventh century had been gaining ground in western Christendom. Its origins go back to the earliest attempts of Christian man to body forth a God in his own image, a reassuring image in times of spiritual anguish. It was with a similar intention that in the middle of the eleventh century the Patarenes of Milan turned their gaze towards the Cross, in which they saw a symbol of victory over death and the powers of evil. The pilgrims who soon after the year 1000 set out for Jerusalem, empty-handed, and whose quest blazed the trail for the crusades, also contributed to the emergence of the Gothic figurations of the Word made flesh. When, on their return from the Holy Land, these men gave eyewitness accounts of Judaea and the Lake of Tiberias and declared that they had touched Christ's tomb with their own hands, and even that they had seen Jesus himself, a tendency developed to impart, little by little, to the face of God the Father the features of the Son of Man, and to give the Son a larger place in the liturgies and chants of the cloisters. As early as 1100 the advocates of church reform had sought to replace the cult of the patriarchs of the Old Dispensation with that of the apostles, and drew spiritual nourishment from the Acts and the Gospel of St Matthew, where stress is laid on poverty. "The various paths to salvation mapped out by the friars, known as the Rules of St Basil, St Augustine and St Benedict, are not the parent stem of the religious life, but grafts inserted in it; not the roots, but foliage. There is but one rule of faith and salvation, a primordial, essential rule, from which all the others flow like streams from the same source, and this is the Holy Gospel which the apostles received from the Saviour Himself. Cling to Christ whose branches you are, and strive in so far as He gives you strength to do so, to conform to the teaching of His Gospel. Thus, when asked about your Rule, your Order, your vocation, answer that you obey the first and fundamental Rule of the Christian life, the Gospels, source and basis of all the Rules." The man who, round about 1150, drew up this prologue to the Rule of Grandmont was putting into words what the most enlightened knights and bourgeois felt, dimly perhaps as yet. Peter Waldo preached the doctrine of Christ as set forth in the Gospels and it was the Master Himself who bade St Francis discard all worldly goods and follow in His steps. Pope Innocent III was convinced that he had received his mandate from the very hands of Jesus and that his deeds were sanctioned by divine authority. The new, profound emotions that were stirring in the hearts of the Christian community—outcome of a raising of the cultural level and a heightened sensibility—account for the placing of the person of the Son of Man, God incarnate, in the forefront of the art of the cathedrals. Catharism may well have owed much of its success to the ambiguities of its vocabulary; its ostensible adhesion to the Gospel message tended to veil its blunt rejection of the Incarnation. By stripping it of such pretenses the Roman Church did away with its appeal to the masses and they now began to turn towards St Francis, who instituted the devotion of the Christchild's Crib *(presepio)* on the night of Christmas. Catholicism triumphed in the Christmas hymns.

In point of fact, however, the theologians who set the course of Gothic art did not visualize Christ as a child but as a king, ruler of the world. In the edifices in whose building the French kings co-operated He was represented as a crowned Doctor and soon was shown seated on a throne crowning the Virgin, his mother but also the Bride: a woman but also the Church. For the churchmen had ended up by justifying, in virtue of the part that Mary had played in the Incarnation, the high place the Mother of God had gradually won for herself in popular esteem during the twelfth century. They endorsed the placing of her image alongside that of Jesus in the heart of their theology, and likewise in the adornment of the cathedrals. And since in the first half of the thirteenth century it was no longer the great ladies of the courts who imposed his themes on the artist and he now conformed to the dictates of the Church, the

king, the bishops and the theologians, he did not express Our Lady's tenderness of heart or her sorrows, but her glory. Ceasing to be an occasion for public rejoicings, the Incarnation became a holy mystery. If sculptors and glass painters placed the image of the Virgin at the most conspicuous points, this was because she signified, for the schoolmen and doctors of the Church, the New Dispensation, fulfilment of the Old. In her person humanity linked up with God; she was the locus of the mystical marriage between the soul and its Creator. And she also gave concrete expression to the idea of a united Church, one and indivisible. For was not the spouse within whom God was made flesh, the Church herself, defender against heresy? Thus the "Coronations of the Virgin" in the cathedrals proclaim, with pomp and circumstance, the indisputable sovereignty of the Church of Rome.

Henceforth the evolution of the Marian iconography kept pace with the images of royal progresses and of the Church triumphant. In 1145 the Royal Portal of Chartres still celebrated the power and the glory of the Romanesque God who figured in the center of the porch, putting to flight the powers of darkness on the Last Day. But, challenging the rising influence of Catharism, it also declared that this God was made flesh, and one of the tympana flanking it contained Gospel scenes relating to the birth of Christ. If the first monumental image of the Mother of God made its appearance in the great city of the Beauce, it was because in this part of France the cult of the Virgin sprang from an ancient tradition going back to Carolingian times and was associated with that upsurge of spirituality in Neustria which had been promoted by the monks and the Frankish kings. Charles the Bald had presented the church of Chartres with some fine pieces of cloth brought from the East, said to be part of the garment Mary was wearing when visited by the archangel Gabriel. Bands of peasants and soldiers flocked to see this holy relic and knelt down before it in pious adoration. Next they were led down to the crypt where there was an effigy of the Virgin in majesty, seated on a throne. When, following Suger's precedent, the sacred relics were transferred from the darkness of underground shrines to the light of day, for all to see, the prelate who made the plans for the Royal Portal had a reproduction in stone of this reliquary statue installed at the center of the scenes of Christ's childhood on the tympanum of the west door. But these figurations were a mere accompaniment to the leading theme: the shepherds, humble compeers of the shepherds of the Ile-de-France, seem dazzled by the splendor of another vision, that of the Mother of God, a timeless, mysterious presence, hieratic here as at Torcello, but seated. For the Virgin also represents "the throne of Solomon, seat of Divinity" that Peter the Venerable was extolling at this very time. A little later the decorators of Laon Cathedral still utilized, in their celebrations of the Virgin, the symbols of the "concordances," Old Testament prefigurations of her immaculacy: the Burning Bush, Gideon's fleece, the Three Holy Children unscathed in the fiery furnace.

The cult of the Virgin was celebrated with an added fervor now that the Church tended more and more to see in her an image of itself. The final step was taken at Senlis in 1190—just when the Church was beginning to stiffen her resistance to heresy—by an emphatic restatement of the doctrine of the Incarnation. Here for the first time an entire cathedral porch was consecrated to the Mother of God. Even her funeral, or rather the transit of her earthly being to celestial glory, was represented. For according to the Oriental beliefs that had infiltrated Latin Christendom, the Virgin did not die but fell asleep, and angels carried her sleeping body up to heaven, sparing her the common lot of mortals. At Senlis Jesus and Mary figured side by side, enthroned, at the summit of the tympanum, and Christ has his mother on his right, signifying that she shares his royalty. Actually this sculpture was simply an illustration of two verses in the liturgy of the Feast of the Assumption: "The queen sits on his right, clad in golden raiment" and "He hath set on her head a crown of precious stones." Launched at the time when Pope Innocent III was claiming universal sovereignty for the Church, this imagery soon came into favor throughout western Christendom. At Notre-Dame in Paris, about 1220, it was given its most perfect interpretation.

Here too, however, it was still relegated to one of the sides of the porch. Thirty years later, when Reims Cathedral was completed, effigies of Mary figured in all parts of the edifice. The original plan drawn up by the master-mason Jean d'Orbais had provided for a porch whose central portion was to contain the patron saints of the cathedral. This plan was modified, these minor intercessors giving place to the supreme mediatrix, the Virgin. In the north portal, to which the patron saints are relegated, she figures in their midst, reinforcing their beneficent activities, and she reappears in the south porch, where her presence intensifies the mystical significance of the apocalyptic vision of the Last Day. Here, as at Senlis, the demonstration of the Christian verities on the front of the cathedral is centered on her person, and she reappears on the mullion of the central door. Monumental representations of the Annunciation, Visitation, Presentation in the Temple and that of King David, her ancestor, bear her company. The moldings of the arches illustrate her life on earth and are also decked with symbolic images of her virginity. Solomon and the Queen of Sheba prefigure her mystical union with Christ the King. To the rose window of the Creation corresponds the western rose depicting her Assumption. And, finally, at the summit of the gable we see Christ with his own hands bestowing on his mother the insignia of sovereign power, the new Adam crowning the new Eve, his spouse. For did He not by his Incarnation ensure the triumph of the Church in this world?

Adam and Jesus, his creator, are like each other. That question which from time immemorial had kept man in awed suspense, pondering on the mystery of the universe and the human predicament—that question "What is God's true visage?"—found an answer in the teachings of the theologians of France : "It is the face of man." In the Royal Portal of Chartres that answer had given rise to the first faint stirrings of life in those Romanesque faces which hitherto had been given an hieratic rigidity, the glacial aloofness of the supramundane. But now a smile rippled on their lips and their gaze lost its trancelike fixity. This new-won life proclaimed itself triumphantly ; sculptors released bodies from the prisoning columns, and gave them the suppleness of natural attitudes under the folds of garments of the heavy cloth then being manufactured in Flanders for the princely courts.

Now that the cathedral porches were used as a stage setting for the liturgical drama and the number of personages figuring in it steadily increased, each had to be plainly recognizable. True, all had distinguishing marks, the attributes assigned by Christian iconography to each prophet, each precursor, every apostle. But a tendency developed to personalize their faces, to make them character-revealing. The vocabulary of the thirteenth-century literature read by the knights was quite inadequate in this respect. Joinville had a genius for describing battles and the brilliant life of royal courts, but grew sadly tongue-tied when it came to delineating a character. For practical purposes, in debates concerning the proper interpretation of feudal rights or details of dress—sometimes, too, in contacts with their confessors—the nobles had gradually sharpened their wits. The schoolmen, needless to say, were versed in self-analysis—this indeed was fundamental to Abelard's conception of morality. For all theology led up to a system of ethics ; it involved soul-searchings and a close study of man's faculties and virtues. And since the doctors of the Church stressed the principle of the oneness of the universe, the intimate connection between the three parts of every human being—body, soul and spirit—, it followed that the traits of a man's face were a visible expression of his personality. Nevertheless the scholastic method aimed at resolving the idiosyncrasies of the individual into forms common to his species and made a point of differentiating between "types." As a result, it is types rather than individuals that the faces of the statues represent.

Many of the cathedrals were built very rapidly and so many figures had to be carved that the work was distributed among several groups of craftsmen. Some were headed by distinguished artists, others by lesser lights. The finest sculptural groups were probably made under the supervision of a master-mason who was responsible for all the building operations and co-ordinated the activities of his subordinates. It would seem that Jean de Chelles himself superintended the execution of the Presentation in the Temple, about 1250, in the porch of the north transept of Notre-Dame in Paris. To a group of sculptors working under Jean d'Orbais, first of the architects of Reims Cathedral, may be assigned most of the statues of saints, apostles and prophets subsequently installed in the large porch. They have affinities both with those in the north portal of Chartres and also—and here the link seems more direct—with figures made by Nicholas of Verdun between 1180 and 1205 for the Klosterneuburg altar, for the shrine of the Magi at Cologne and that of the Virgin at Tournai. Some of the statues, however—those of Mary and Elizabeth in the group of the Visitation, those of Gabriel and some prophets—, are treated in an unusual manner; their garments have just the same type of folds as those of the veils with which classical Greek sculptors draped their goddesses. Are we to assume that after the crusade of 1204 Hellenic models had a direct influence on the sculpture of the West? In point of fact the chief innovation here consists in the lifelike movement given the bodies, a movement like that of the Victories of Greek statuary, which dispenses with frontality and sweeps them forward. In the atelier of Jean Le Loup, between 1228 and 1233, were made the statues of the Virgin, of the Annunciation and the Presentation, of Solomon, the Queen of Sheba and Philip Augustus. They resemble those of Amiens, but are more expressive; they have an unwonted suppleness and grace, and the faces convey new shades of feeling.

About 1237 the layout of the Reims decorations was taken over in toto at Bamberg, where bishop Egbert, brother-in-law of King Philip of France, was starting building operations. On the choir screen of St George an unknown master represented Jonah and Hosea engaged in a heated controversy like two doctors of the Church. Rendered with a startling veracity, they seem charged with the dauntless energy of the pioneer explorers of the German backwoods, the missionaries and the early crusaders, inspired by the heroic faith of Parsifal.

THE PROPHETS JONAH AND HOSEA, ABOUT 1240.
RELIEFS ON THE CHOIR SCREEN OF BAMBERG CATHEDRAL.

144

THE PRESENTATION IN THE TEMPLE, ABOUT 1250.
SCULPTURE IN THE PORTAL OF THE NORTH TRANSEPT, CATHEDRAL OF NOTRE-DAME, PARIS.

ADAM, DETAIL OF A STATUE FROM BAMBERG CATHEDRAL. ABOUT 1240. DIOCESAN MUSEUM, BAMBERG.

MAIDSERVANT, DETAIL OF A STATUE ON THE FAÇADE OF REIMS CATHEDRAL. ABOUT 1240.

5

THE VIRGIN
AND THE RESURRECTED

Historians are at a loss for the underlying reasons of the change that took place when the martyrs and confessors to whom the cathedrals of France had formerly been dedicated were replaced by Our Lady, who thus became the sole and common patron of them all. There are grounds, however, for surmising that the sudden rise of the cult of Mary in the Gothic age—like the evangelical revival which had preceded it, like the eremitical monasticism of the first Carthusians, like the asceticism of Citeaux and so many other religious movements which since the end of the eleventh century had inspired new forms of imagery—was a result of the contacts of Latin Christianity with the East. For at this time the Byzantine establishment had more initiative, more creative energy, and more resources to draw on than that of France or Germany. All the great shrines of the Virgin were in the East. Embroidering on the rather scanty references to her in the Gospels and the Acts and eking them out with anecdotes of their own invention, Byzantine monks had built up an elaborate Marian iconography. It was there that the legend of the "Dormition" originated; Mary had not died, God would not let his spouse and mother suffer the indignity of physical decay. She fell asleep and her sleeping body was wafted to the celestial realm by a company of angels. Henceforth she sits enthroned in highest heaven on the right of God,

Son and Father. Thus she occupies an all-glorious place in the Kingdom of God, at the apex of the celestial hierarchy, immediately beside the Supreme Source of light and goodness. She is the highest dignitary in the court of heaven and Our Lord hearkens to her counsels. Full of loving-kindness for all men and compassion for their lapses, she pleads for them and welcomes them at their journey's end. Like her, all men and women will one day win through to the Light. Illustrated by the sculptors in Paris and Senlis, this tale of the Dormition encouraged preachers to stress the note of hope, that prospect of a glad resurrection of which her presence in the court of heaven gave a warranty.

People always felt death very near them in the thirteenth century. It is impossible for us today to form any clear idea of the fears that tormented the minds of all those peasants who never ate their fill and were forever at the mercy of epidemics or armed marauders. But we know more of the mentality of the nobility for whom courage ranked first in their code of honor and who were so often the prey of that most potent of emotions: fear. The knights took heart when they listened in some great hall to a minstrel singing the exploits of Roland or William of Orange, defender of the South against the Moslems, but they were full of dark forebodings when they embarked on ships sailing to the Holy Land or took part in tournaments where they had, turn by turn, to enter the lists and gallop at each other, lance in hand. The great advances made in the crafts of armor and fortification were an outcome of this fear, and it had a large part in the religion of the day. To how many of these men did church-going, touching sacred relics, joining in the liturgy, making the ritual gestures, mean more than palliatives of the haunting fear of death?

All were surrounded by the dead; the solidarity of a family was not embodied only in gatherings of the living members of the clan. The present generation felt itself linked to its innumerable forbears; their names and exploits were constantly recalled, and sometimes their phantasms visited the living in their dreams. Every knight was profoundly conscious of his lineage; the family tree had its roots in an array of tombs above which memorial services were regularly held. When he felt his end approach-

ing, or when about to take part in some particularly dangerous venture, he gave thought to acts of piety and propitiation and donated to the priests and monasteries a share of his worldly goods, hoping to win the favor of the saints and make his peace with God. In short the chief concern of a man's life, the object of his most anxious thought and heaviest expenditure, was to forearm himself against the last enemy, death.

However the religion we see illustrated in the art of the cathedrals was not the religion of the masses. It was that of a small intellectual élite whose fervent faith enabled them to overcome their very human fears, to bathe their souls in the spiritual light, and to feel assured of a joyous resurrection. Christ had vanquished death—why then fear it? Each new dawn brought back the promise of the first Easter day when its rays fell on the tympanum where tier by tier the drama of the Last Judgment was enacted, a vision of all men rising from their graves, like the end of a bad dream. The shades of night fell from their faces and their eyes opened; casting off their shrouds, they bared perfect bodies to the rising light and entered into the true life.

When it became a practice to decorate the tombs of kings and prelates and to place on each an effigy of the dead man, the cathedral authorities insisted that this "likeness" should be sublimated, stylized. The tomb statues of Bishop Evrard de Fouilloy at Lyons and Henry the Lion at Brunswick might equally well have figured in the porches, among the effigies of prophets. The garments do not drape a corpse recumbent on a deathbed but a standing man, his eyes wide open, gazing at the celestial light. Like those of Solomon and King David, their faces are calm and confident, unwrinkled, without blemish. Had not St Augustine written "God made Himself man so that we men might become like gods"? In virtue of his Incarnation and Resurrection Christ himself had blazed the trail leading all mortals to the heavenly Father and, since death is only a passing phase and the tomb but a place of germination where each human being undergoes a transformation preparatory to the glorious after-life, the art of the cathedrals shows the dead Christian's body already invested with the perfect form it will have for all eternity in its celestial abode.

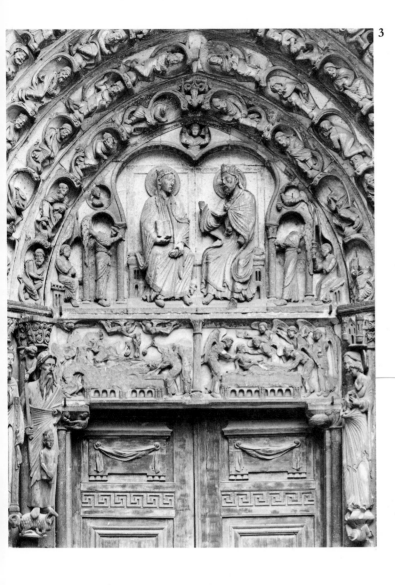

3

4

155

THE REDEMPTION

In the image of the Creation and the Incarnation devised by the thirteenth-century theologians, the universe, ceasing to bear the stamp of guilt, had also ceased to terrify. It now seemed clear—anyhow to that section of the Christian community which was learning to profit by the new "enlightenment"—that sin could not be atoned for by rites apportioned to the gravity of the offence, just as that the miraculous decision of the "ordeal" was no sure test of the guilt or innocence of a man accused of a crime. The thirteenth-century Christian knew that salvation must be achieved by deeds and, still more, by intentions, by the love and understanding that made him feel he was at one with God, led him back to his Maker and to a more perfect imitation of Christ. True, sin still existed; it cast its shadow on all material things and obstructed the passage of the Light Divine. Jesus alone had vanquished it, and He alone could free man from its thrall. Therefore it was the Christian's duty to follow the Good Master and learn, like Him, to bear his cross.

This was the message broadcast by all the mendicant friars. "Do not speak to me," St Francis said, "of any other way of life than the one which Our Lord Himself has mercifully vouchsafed to show me. The Rule of the Friars Minor consists in obeying the Holy Gospels of our Lord Christ Jesus"—the Gospels in their stark simplicity, *sine glossa*, without any comment. St Dominic, too, claimed to be first and foremost "a follower of the Gospels." But the preaching of the Truth, though it now allowed for joy, laid stress on penitence. It urged the Christian to further his progress by accepting in his body the sufferings of the Passion. This was the lot of St Francis on Mount Alverno. "Some time before his death our brother and father was seen having marks on his body which were truly the Stigmata of the Crucified... At the first hour of the day Francis knelt down and stretching out his arms as on a cross and gazing towards the East, addressed this prayer to the Saviour. 'O Lord Jesus, there are two favors I beg Thee to grant before my death. First that, so far as this is possible, I may suffer the same pangs as thou, my gentle Jesus, didst suffer in thy cruel Passion. And, secondly, that I may feel, so far as possible, in my heart that boundless love which burnt in Thee, O Son of God, and which led Thee to endure willingly so many pains on behalf of us, miserable sinners.'" When fifty years later King St Louis wished to follow the same path, it was (as Joinville relates) "because he loved God with all his heart and imitated His deeds; this is proved by the fact that just as Our Lord died for the sake of His people, so our saintly king risked his life time and again out of love for his." For those who shared in the new affluence the thirteenth century was an age of spectacular progress, ever-increasing enjoyment of the good things of the earth. But calls to penitence, warnings not to stray from the path leading to the Promised Land, kept pace, step by step, with this advance. Like the guides of the crusaders, the sculpture in the cathedrals bore the sign of the cross. It teemed with images of the Passion. But this imagery also contained symbols of Christ's victory, proclaimed that God made man had Himself crossed the valley of death, and called on all mankind to follow Him to the abode of true joys, not to be found on earth.

In its glorification of a God who had suffered and died, Latin Christendom followed a trend of thought long current in the East. From the eleventh century on, Byzantine prelates had taught their flocks to see in the rites of the Mass a concrete reminder of Christ's death, burial and resurrection. The liturgy of the Eastern Church dramatized all the incidents of the Saviour's life. The Communion service was an epitome of the Gospel narrative, of which the Macedonian frescoes gave a visual transcription. Soon, too, reflections of these images made their appearance at Cefalù. The crusaders saw these figures on their way to the Holy Land, where they discovered a "real" Jerusalem, more immediately convincing than the eschatological symbols which had fired the imagination of the Western Christians in 1095. The storming of Constantinople in 1204 by Frankish warriors was an epochal event; it was hoped that the schism would soon be healed and the two severed portions of Christ's body reunited in a truly catholic church. What this victory actually did was to give the West an opportunity of seizing all the relics of the Passion preserved in the churches of Constantinople. Robert de Clary (chronicler of *La Prise de Constantinople*) gazed with awe-struck wonder at these treasures: fragments of the True Cross, the head of the lance that pierced the Saviour's side, two nails, the Crown of Thorns. And the sight of the instruments of the Passion lifted it out of a world of dreams into a vivid actuality. The knights bought or pillaged systematically all the precious relics; Count Baldwin of Flanders even brought back to his castle at Ghent some alleged drops of Christ's blood. For many centuries the West had cherished with naive faith the objects, often of dubious origin, preserved in abbey crypts. The authenticity of those brought back by the crusaders seemed better assured and they were given shrines in keeping with their unique sanctity. Old chapels were refurbished, new ones built. "King St Louis owned the Crown of Thorns and a large piece of the Holy Cross on which Our Lord was crucified; also the lance that wounded Him and many other sacred relics. To enshrine them he built the Sainte-Chapelle in Paris at a cost of over forty thousand livres minted at Tours. He decorated with gold and precious stones and other pieces of jewelry the places and the reliquaries containing the holy relics and it is said that these embellishments were worth a hundred thousand livres and more." Above each reliquary was a figurative ornament indicating the origin, significance and special properties of the sacred object preserved in it. Thus the vogue for decoration which developed in the first half of the thirteenth century was a direct outcome of the sack of Constantinople.

To do honor to the newly acquired relics, artists had to use their imagination. The art of Byzantium had employed type forms appropriate to the Old Dispensation. Now the emphasis shifted to the New and it was felt that the sufferings of Christ should be given less abstract expression. Accordingly the authorities drawing up the new artistic programs prescribed the use of themes of a more emotive order, culled from the Gospels. For the most urgent need was to convince the masses, and the Church Militant, in its campaign against heresy, sought to strike home to the hearts of the populace at large. (A similar recourse to Gospel themes had been practised several generations earlier by the eastern artists.) Hence the frequent illustrations in sculpture and stained-glass of scenes of the Passion. In the sketchbook of Villard de Honnecourt we see Nicodemus unnailing the feet of Christ, and the original project for the Reims porch was modified to include —for the first time on a cathedral portal—a representation of the Crucifixion. For the same purpose the alterations made by Suger in the rendering of the Last Judgment were carried a stage further, with the result that its significance was totally changed. At Chartres the Christ of the Second Coming is not represented as a triumphant monarch, but given the humble aspect of a man who has greatly suffered; He displays His wounds and is surrounded by the instruments of the Passion, the lance, the crown of thorns and the beams of the cross. Nevertheless these instruments are not carried by His executioners or by Christ Himself, but by angels who hold them forth like holy relics and dare not even touch them with their hands—they are wrapped in fine linen. For the theologian who devised this scene did not aim primarily at stressing the Saviour's physical suffering, still less the mutilation of His body. For him the cross was not a gibbet, rather a sign of glory, and the wounds of Jesus do not betoken His agony. "They proclaim His strength," Thomas Aquinas said, "for He vanquished death."

At this time the doctors of the Church were less preoccupied with Good Friday than with the joyous victory of Easter. At Reims, at the back of the portal where windows were installed so that here too light should enter freely, the representations of the Redemption are surrounded by flowers and fruit and vineyards. The figures, too, are real persons, not symbols; however they are not just actors in a drama. The purpose of these statues is to represent the spiritual values of which the Crucifixion was the sign and to suggest its eucharistic correspondences. Since thirteenth-century Christendom was more than ever ecclesiastic and in its war against the heretics exalted the functions of the priesthood, and since Gothic art was, in fact, created by the priests, the statues of Reims were shown as celebrants of the Eucharist, the sacrament which elevated ministers of the Catholic Church far above the Cathar "Perfecti" and Waldensian preachers. They transposed that supreme event, the death of Jesus, into the eternity of the rites of the Church and a supernal peace. Above their serene company, at the level of the rose (where about 1260 the iconographic plan concluded), the row of kings provided for in the initial project was replaced, at the last moment, by another group, that of the persons who saw the risen Christ after His Resurrection. They proclaimed in the heights, at the climax of the upward-surging movement of the great cathedral, Christ's victory over death and bade all Christians rejoice in it. Implicit in their message was a promise of redemption. Well aware that even faithful Christians were haunted by a dread of the after-life, the Church assured them of their ultimate salvation. What was offered was something more effective than the Cathar rite of the *consolamentum*; for those who took refuge in the bosom of the Church the passage from darkness into light need have no terrors. St Francis had hymned the praises of "our sister, bodily death, which no living man can escape; unhappy are they alone who die in mortal sin, and blessed are those who have performed their Master's very holy will, for then the second death will not afflict them." In virtue of the Resurrection death has lost its sting.

The Church allowed the great men of the age to install their tombs in churches and to set up above them their likenesses in stone. Round about 1200 there began, in the oratory of the Templars in London, the long cortège of recumbent tomb effigies. At Saint-Denis St Louis decided to use Suger's basilica as a royal mausoleum enshrining the fune-rary monuments of his forbears, and gave Peter of Montreuil orders to this effect. With this in mind he arrayed the tombs in the transept crossing, like so many beds for lying-in-state. But he did not place on them effigies of corpses; instead, he set up column-statues with faces having the serene anonymity of those of the Kings of Judah. For in the timeless realm beyond the grave did not these French kings and queens have their appointed place in the "earthly" lineage of the Son of Man? And in the eyes of the Eternal Father to whom a thousand years are as a day, surely Christ's Passion and Resurrection signified but a phase of ever-rolling Time? For these were still prefigurations, incidents in the history of signs and symbols; the resurrection of all men existed for all eternity in its archetype, Christ's resurrection. The death of an individual man signalized no more than the return of light to its first principle, of the created being to its divine source. This is why the recumbent tomb effigies of the thirteenth century seem ageless, their faces so impersonal. Rid of all accidentals, they have reverted to the specific type-form, that of God incarnate; the ecstasy to which St Bernard aspired finds visible embodiment at last in these stately figures. At Reims the Resurrected, arising from their sepulchres charged with vibrant life, have the very aspect of the Son of Man, of Christ showing His wounded hands and side, yet resplendent with the light of godhead, of the Creator. Thus Man's destiny, his long progress, with its setbacks and its triumphs, culminates in the Redemption. But both the Redemption and the Creation are summed up in the Incarnation.

Within the cathedral the stained-glass workers transposed the didactic imagery of the porch into a world of light. The moment he crossed the threshold, the Christian drew a step nearer to an apprehension of the vera lux. *Become a son of God in virtue of the Incarnation, he shared in the heritage of divine illumination. He entered that interspace which, as Suger had pointed out, has its true being neither in gross earth nor as yet in the purity of heaven, but where already God speaks to man in a supernal radiance.*

Given the number of windows, the task of filling them with decorations in stained glass called for a large labor force. Many teams of workers were employed, not all of them up to the highest standard. Hence the occasional lapses in the quality of the composition and the sureness of the linework in the Sainte-Chapelle. But these flaws pass unnoticed, so potent is the magic of these richly glowing colors, so strong their grip on our emotions. Here we see put in practice the aesthetic of William of Auvergne. "This invisible beauty is a consequence either of the shape or the position of the parts within a whole; or else of the color, or else of two of these factors combined, whether by being juxtaposed, or in virtue of harmonious relations associating each with each." Colors are chosen not with an eye to faithfully copying natural appearances, but in view of their interrelations on the luminous ground forming their support. Like Pérotin le Grand's polyphony, the stained-glass window blends together an infinite variety of rhythms and modulations, often discordant inter se. *It effects a transformation of the visible, building up a world of strange enchantments.*

The lower stained-glass windows narrate; they supply the data of a doctrinal thesis on the lines of a professional lecture. The seminal text, the message, is located in the central medallion; beside and around it are subsidiary figurations culled from the Bible, which by an interplay of complementary allusions help the beholder to comprehend its purport, and to proceed from its literal to its mystical significance. And since this demonstration follows the rules of scholastic logic, the imagery proves, in visual terms, the strict coherence of the Christian dogma.

On the windows of the choir of Saint-Denis Suger had disposed a series of allegorical scenes, for understanding which "the anagogical approach" was essential. However, he had combined with these some easily understood scenes of the life of Jesus. In the twelfth-century cathedral the windows were filled even more profusely than the porches with an iconography immediately deriving from the Gospels. But they tell little of the public life of Christ and nothing of His miracles. Almost all the motifs relate to His childhood and Passion, as described in the Gospels of the Easter and Christmas services.

THE THREE MAGI AND THE FLIGHT INTO EGYPT, ABOUT 1215. STAINED-GLASS WINDOW IN THE APSE OF LAON CATHEDRAL.

MAN IN THE STAINED-GLASS WINDOW

At Bourges ten low windows arranged in pairs couple scenes with a didactic purpose: the demonstration of certain fundamental correspondences. Here with a wealth of colored signs the Passion confronts the Apocalypse, and the New Covenant the Last Judgment. In the upper part of the cathedral, however, large isolated figures occupy the bays. Arrayed around the choir a cortège of prophets on the north, of apostles on the south, converge on the image of the Virgin (standing for the Church) and proclaim, with a monumental simplicity, the unity of history and Christian dogma, and the concordance between the Old and the New Testaments. At Chartres the same prophets, surrounded by saints, carry on their shoulders the apostles. Daily the first rays of the rising sun bathe in light, above the darkness of the carnal world, these unsleeping guardians of the Faith. Here the almost garish profusion of colors investing the Gospel scenes and the complex figurations of analogies in the lower registers of the edifice is toned down. The figures in these austerely colored windows are the figures of men, men who had lived on earth but here are charged with power and majesty.

Most are the saints whose reliquaries were housed in the cathedral, where the store of relics had been recently enriched by a variety of holy objects brought from the East. In 1206 a portion of the head of St John the Baptist had been presented to Amiens and a stained-glass window was dedicated to him; he had another in the Sainte-Chapelle where the back of his skull was preserved. Chartres had a St Anne window, Sens a St Thomas à Becket window. Ferdinand of Castile presented Chartres with the St James window, St Louis with that of St Denis. These contained depictions of their coats-of-arms, and sometimes figures of the donors were included among the prophets. In the Reims windows Archbishop Henri de Braisne gave orders for the façades of his metropolitan cathedral and the seven provincial cathedrals to be represented under the images of Christ. Symbolic emblems associated these cathedrals with the "seven churches in Asia" mentioned in the Book of Revelation and with "the angels of the seven churches" who received Christ's message. The archbishop also had himself represented with his suffragans grouped around him as in a feudal court. At the very time when the Church was stressing the doctrine of the Incarnation and Gothic genius came to its full flowering, human pride was beginning to rear its head in the realm of the celestial glories, in the upper windows of the cathedral and, on its front, in the stately rows of kings.

ST DENIS HANDING THE ORIFLAMME TO CLEMENT OF METZ. 13TH CENTURY.
STAINED-GLASS WINDOW IN THE SOUTH TRANSEPT OF CHARTRES CATHEDRAL.

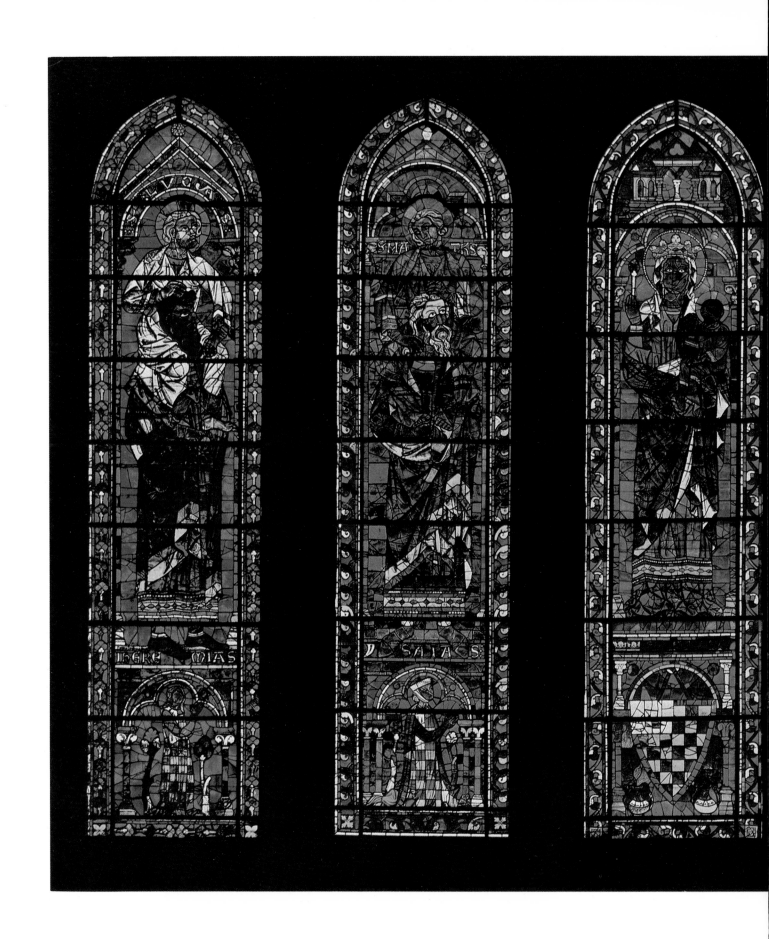

STAINED-GLASS WINDOWS UNDER
THE ROSE WINDOW OF THE SOUTH TRANSEPT.
13TH CENTURY. CHARTRES CATHEDRAL.

169

III

MAN
1250-1280

THE PERILS OF THE NEW AGE

It was in the university of Paris that the most effective weapons in the fight against heresy were forged. Most of the prelates of Christendom—the bishops of Scandinavia, of Hungary, of the Morea, St Jean d'Acre, Nicosia and many other parts of Europe—and the popes themselves, its patrons, were educated in this famous university. The students had joined the triumphal procession in which the prisoners taken at Bouvines were exhibited in cages to the exultant populace. After his resounding defeat of the Emperor, the King of France assumed the surname of "Augustus" and reigned supreme in the West. To the laurels of the French crown Louis IX added the aureole of sainthood. St Louis had an uncontested moral authority; he was the master of Languedoc and it was under his auspices that the inquisitors strove to eradicate the last traces of heresy in that region. His brother ruled Provence, Naples and Sicily and the thrones of Europe looked to him for guidance. He sought to give his nobles an example of the "new chivalry": of the ideal knight, valiant in battle, devout but capable of lighter moods and courteous to ladies. We get an idea of the king's face from the famous statue of a horseman at Bamberg. All the élite of Christendom aspired to speak his language. Meanwhile the sensuality of the troubadours, the extravagances of the Breton romances were giving place to the crystal-clear vision and gracious allegories of the first *Roman de la Rose*. Thanks to its famous university and sainted king Paris—and with Paris the art of France—held pride of place in thirteenth-century Europe.

This art had conquered new provinces, those which had been incorporated one by one in the royal domain (Normandy, Artois, Anjou) or, like Champagne, Burgundy and Flanders, had recognized the overlordship of the French king. The bishops had introduced at Trondheim, in Castile and in Franconia, notions in conformity with the tenets of the best contemporary theology; these they had acquired while studying in Paris. Dominicans and Franciscans had recently taken over the ideas originally formulated by the Cistercians and were giving them wide currency; the basilica at Assisi and the Minerva in Rome are Gothic churches. The struggle against heresy had broken down most of the barriers impeding the advance of the aesthetic of the French churches; imposed by force on the subjugated South, at Toulouse and Clermont, it was soon to make good in all the citadels of Catharism, at Limoges, Bayonne and Narbonne. Assimilating what was best in rival schools of art, French sculptors were adorning their works with these new-found acquisitions. In the statuary of Reims were forms borrowed from Roman sarcophagi, from Mosan baptismal fonts and from antique cameos, replicas of which were being produced in Paris. And today art historians are seeking to trace the debt these sculptors may well have owed to Greece herself.

Nevertheless from the middle of the century on, there was a feeling in Paris, headquarters of the now triumphant aesthetic, that a far-reaching change was impending, a change that was to transform the whole aspect of the visible world. Most of the work in the Sainte-Chapelle was terminated in 1248; on Notre-Dame in 1250; on Amiens in 1269; the large-scale sculpture at Reims was completed in 1260. And, as it so happened, this last-named year was precisely the one which according to Abbot Joachim of Floris in his prophetic *Expositio in Apocalypsin* was due to mark a turning point in history, and to usher in the Third Age of humanity. After the Age of the Father and that of the Son was to come the Age of the Spirit, when, as announced in the Apocalypse, the Eternal Gospel would prevail and a golden age begin in which all Christians would lead lives of joyous poverty and there would be no more need for a prelacy. Entirely consisting of monks and saints, the whole human race would form a new Church, purified, pervaded by the Spirit. Joachim's books were widely read and many began to see in St Francis the harbinger of this age of enlightenment. A Franciscan theologian, Gerard of Borgo San Donnino, lectured on the works of Joachim in the university of Paris. He had an opponent in another learned professor, Guillaume de Saint-Amour, who soon after 1250 wrote a treatise *Concerning the Perils of the New Age*, in which he denounced the preaching friars as "false prophets" wantonly competing with the lay teachers of the university, and even attacked the pope, patron of the mendicant Orders.

What Guillaume was expressing was in effect the reaction of the modern world to the Church's severe restrictions on progressive thought. This revolt took various forms, chief of them a protest against the tyranny of the papal "monarchy" and those who served it. The Holy See wished to dominate the world, to rule it with a rod of iron. It had already set upon the pope's tiara a second crown with fleurons, the crown of the kings of the earth, symbol of imperial power. For the Church claimed universal sovereignty as a legacy from Constantine the Great. Conquered Byzantium was garrisoned by Catholic knights and the pope had defeated the emperor Frederick II. When Frederick died, in 1250, the Curia did not appoint a successor and there ensued an interregnum. For the pope was determined to rule alone. He claimed unrestricted dominion throughout the length and breadth of Christendom, this being essential, he said, for the stamping out of heresy. In 1252 with this in mind Innocent IV authorized the use of torture by the inquisitors. Still, it was clear enough by then that the repression had done its work. Montségur had fallen, no avowed Cathar existed anywhere. The aim of this centralization of power in the Holy See was both to safeguard its temporal interests and to satisfy the worldly ambition of the cardinals. Surrendering to the materialist temptation against which St Bernard had warned her, Rome had become "the slave of Mammon." Some even saw in Rome the harlot of the Apocalypse, and Dante may have been thinking of this when he exclaimed (*Inferno*, XIX):

> Ah, Constantine, how great were the evils mothered
> Not by thy conversion but by that marriage-dower
> Which the first wealthy pontiff got from thee!

Central to the millennial prophecies of Joachim was an abhorrence of the papal tyranny. The golden epoch he dreamt of and whose coming he predicted (for 1260) was to be the age of the Holy Spirit, when there would be no more need for priests. In 1252 the Holy See forbade the reading of *The Eternal Gospel*. But already in southern Christendom, where though the Cathar heresy had been eradicated, the ferment of the spirit of poverty still was operative, many Franciscans were beginning to rebel against the Roman hierarchy and to preach spiritual freedom and the imitation of the Poverello. At Hyères, on his way back from the crusade, St Louis had heard a mendicant friar declaiming against the monks who were leading pampered lives under the aegis of the royal court. Joinville was among the audience and he was equally against these "canting hypocrites" —though for different reasons. Because, for one thing, they chided him for his "vain display," and also because the bishop's men were enlarging their judicial powers at his expense, within his own domain. This antagonism to the established Church was developing chiefly in the vital centers of the kingdoms, the nationalistic States into which Europe was now in course of being divided. For, like the Italian communes and thirteenth-century Rome, Christendom as a whole was beginning to split up into self-contained, hostile units, fortresses from which every great power watched its rivals and made ready to attack them. The time of great wars was approaching, the unity symbolized by the "seamless garment" of the crowned Virgin in the cathedrals was coming to seem a myth and the New Jerusalem a shadowy hope having no real substance. Reality in 1250 was embodied in the secular State and its increasing horde of petty officials eager to defend the prerogatives of their employer since these ensured their own prestige. Among some of these servants of the princes one saw stirrings of the temerity which was soon to lead a man like Guillaume de Nogaret to slap a pope's face—on behalf of the king of France! Already in the mid-thirteenth century every monarch claimed to be master in his own house and mocked at the temporal pretensions of the papacy. Even St Louis, ready to serve Christ but not the bishop of Rome, espoused the cause of that arch-zealously anticlerical Frederick II and defended his own vassals against encroachments of the Church's jurisdiction.

The resistance of the contemporary world to ecclesiastical constraints was a result of the new, progressive spirit of the age and of the increasing prosperity of the West. There was also a revival of dissatisfaction with what remained of the old feudal system. While the poorer classes became more and more resentful of their lot, the well-to-do rebelled against the doctrine of abstinence from worldly joys preached by the Church. The messianic visions of men like Abbot Joachim and a vague hope of a golden age in which all men would regain the equality of the first days of the world were affecting the mentality of the submerged masses: workers in the suburbs of the larger cities (among whom heresy still lurked), the cloth-makers, the "blue fingernails" who in 1280 launched the first strikes known to history. Soon the movement spread to the depths of the country and there were sporadic outbreaks when some rebellious monk or fanatic visionary claiming divine inspiration mustered the forces of revolt. Bands of credulous peasants set forth in quest of a deliverer, an earthly incarnation of the Saviour, pillaging on their way the granaries of the Church. Such was the Shepherds' Crusade, a "religious Jacquerie" led by the so-called Master of Hungary, whose followers roved the countryside of the Ile-de-France, proclaiming their intention to rescue the good king of France from the hands of the infidels who had taken him captive. These vagrant, poverty-stricken hordes saw in the pope and the bishops, who blessed their persecutors and incited the knights to drown their revolt in blood and to destroy their vague but noble hope, the emissaries of Antichrist. Nobles, pope, bishops and even the mendicant friars regarded as mere trouble-makers these "Pastoureaux" who sought to rob well-born folk of the wealth which God had seen fit to bestow on them and who refused to be consoled for present ills by promises of a happy after-life. In one of the most charming of the romances of the period young Aucassin fears to be bored in paradise and to find in it no more pleasure than he does in the priests' litanies; if fair ladies have to go to hell, he prefers to follow them there!

Meanwhile another dream was being shattered by harsh reality: the dream of a coming millennium when the whole world was to be united in the Christian faith. All Europe, after the early successes of the war with Islam, had shared this dream—there was now a rude awakening. This disillusionment seems to have led to the most insidious malady of the age: the feeling that the images of a well-ordered Creation, conformant to God's plan, that figured in the cathedrals were not to be taken at their face value. Jerusalem, which meant so much to the crusaders,

had not been delivered; in 1190 they had failed to recapture the Holy Sepulchre. During the long siege of Acre they had learned that among the Saracens, too, there were "very parfit knights" and, saddest of all, they had returned in an inglorious plight, sick and empty-handed. They set forth again, but this time turned against fellow Christians, the "dissenters" of Southern France; then, guided by Italian traders, looted Constantinople. St Louis himself was captured and forced to pay a ransom; he was unable to complete his pilgrimage to the tomb of Christ. In 1261 schismatics expelled the Franks from Constantinople. St Louis tried once again to lead his vassals to the Holy Land. In the result the crusade came to nothing and St Louis sickened and died a month after it had started. "In my opinion," Joinville said, "all who urged the king to make this expedition were guilty of mortal sin." None the less Latin bishops, monks and colonists stayed on in the Levant and generations of knights were still to dream of new crusades. But the first fine zest had gone; the noble hope of a reunion of all the Christian nations at the Holy Sepulchre was ended. The armies of the West had ceased to advance. They were first held, then thrust back, by superior forces, one outpost after another was abandoned, and Europe herself imperilled. Western man was growing conscious of the immensity of Asia, the vast reservoir of man-power on which his enemies could draw and the ominous analogies with the age preceding the fall of the Roman Empire. He saw Mongol hordes pouring down from the steppes and when in 1241 and 1243 Polish and Hungarian Christians had to struggle desperately against these wild men with strange faces they thought to see in them the hosts of Gog and Magog or the Horsemen of the Apocalypse, harbingers of the day of doom.

The leaders of the Church were thus made aware that only a relatively small part of the world had been christianized; it was no longer possible to believe that it was only a question of time—perhaps a short time—for all mankind to be converted to the true faith. The culture of the thirteenth-century churchman was far ahead of that of his predecessors and he could not fail to recognize the fact that the created world was far vaster, more diverse and less docile than used to be supposed. It teemed with people who had never heard the word of God, who shut their ears to it, and conquering whom by arms was no light task. Henceforth there was no more talk in Europe of "holy wars." An age of explorers, traders, missionaries was now setting in. Why persist in fighting the infidels, doughty warriors all? Would it not be wiser to negotiate, to try to gain a foothold in those unconquerable kingdoms by peaceful trading, and on occasion preaching? In 1271 Marco Polo set out on the Silk Road, after getting from Venetian merchants, his compatriots, and from mendicant friars a description of the route to follow. The dynamism of the knights of France was replaced by the new dynamism of the Italian merchant-adventurers. Moreover a close study of the Gospels was making clearer every day how barbarous it was, indeed how contrary to Christ's teaching, to wish to exterminate the heathens or, as in the days of Charlemagne, to force them, under pain of death, to be baptized. No, the right thing was to talk to them, to familiarize them with the Christian way of life. The prelates had discarded Turpin's helm and many of them now wore the Franciscan homespun robe. At Damietta St Francis had seen for himself that, morally, the crusaders were little better than their adversaries and stood in no less need of being converted. With some of the Little Brothers he had ventured into the no-man's-land between the camps, got himself taken prisoner and openly preached the Gospel to the sultan—without any immediate success. But a new hope was dawning; it was learnt that Nestorian Christian communities still existed in little-known parts of Asia ruled by Tartar khans. Since the Mongols left the Christians in peace, they seemed more likely converts to the true faith than were the Moslems, the common enemy. They were regarded, in fact, as gentle savages; not as precursors of "the scourge of God" but as potential allies, who might help by taking the Moslem armies in the rear. A Franciscan mission actually set out to convert the "savages." St Louis sent the Asian chiefs "a set of vestments and altar-cloths in scarlet so as to win them to our faith. On these fabrics were images of the Annunciation, the Nativity, the Baptism of Our Lord, the entire Passion, the Ascension and the Coming of the Holy Spirit. Also the king sent chalices, books, all things needful for the service of the Mass, and two preaching friars to intone it in their presence." Europe was no longer sending out men of arms but the best of its preachers, and pictures to illustrate their sermons—all the new imagery of the cathedrals. Unfortunately these spiritual weapons were no more successful than the others. Christendom was still limited to a small portion of the world.

After 1250, at the very time when the western Christian was learning his relativity in space, he also discovered the relativity of Christian history. Until now Time had been conceived of as an homogeneous whole in which, conforming to the divine exemplar, past and future were coherent with the present, bound to it by some mystical relationship. *Sub specie aeternitatis* the moment of creation and that of the world's end were indistinguishable and the present moment was included in them. St Augustine and the Pseudo-Areopagite had expressed this view of Time. It was fundamental to Suger's "concordances," the Biblical paradigms of Peter "the Devourer," and the entire symbolic schema in which the art of the cathedrals reduced Time to the cosmic gyre of the rose windows. Past events do not explain the present but prefigure and complement it.

But in the second half of the thirteenth century there were signs that this conception of Time was losing its authority. Humbert of Romans, master-general of the Dominicans, was instructed by the pope to look into the history of the Greek schism. Plans were made for a council for reuniting the eastern and western churches, and the discussions were to be given an historical basis—a quite new departure. In his *Treatise in Three Parts* (1273) Humbert sought to discover reasons—not only supernatural reasons—for the present state of affairs. Ceasing to concentrate on the mystical correspondences assumed to exist between the facts of history and the contents of the Book of Revelation, he aimed at ascertaining the *real* relations between these facts, the links between them and their material and psychological context. Thus Humbert's attitude to history was diametrically opposed to that of Joachim of Floris; the Age of the Spirit was not to come in the future, it was over, and the present age pertained to the Church. This attitude clearly ruled out any conception of Time as a tissue of recurring patterns. The march of history was a constructive movement, guided by the urge which, in Humbert's youth, had activated culture and the building of cathedrals in the Ile-de-France. Humbert has much to tell of the optimism of the builders and architects, of the enthusiasm of the mendicant friars who, far from dreaming the hours away in a cloister, went out into the world, and even took to learning Arabic so as to convert the infidels of Islam. But the author was not blind to the difficulties and setbacks these missionaries would encounter. He had lived many years among the counsellors of St Louis, had witnessed the defeated king's return, the tragic issue of his new venture, the fall of the Emperor Frederick, then that of the Latin Empire of Constantinople. He goes so far as to say that the "Greeks" are not heretics but estranged brothers of the western Christians, and that not they alone were responsible for this separation. He has ceased to believe in the unity of Christendom, even indeed in its necessity; he sees it as contingent, relative, a purely human concept.

And, lastly, Humbert, like all the best thinkers of the day, was well aware that the eastern schism, Islam, the heathen peoples of Asia did not constitute the only coherent religious denominations outside the pale of the western Church. Confronted by Greek and Arab modes of thought, European intellectuals were compelled to recognize the relativity of their theology. Here was a disconcerting discovery and one which clearly, and in a fundamental manner, called in question the world of the cathedrals. The pontifical embargo on the study of Aristotle in the schools (except his works on logic) had proved ineffective. Albertus Magnus had no hesitation about lecturing on natural philosophy and in 1252 the English section included in the curriculum for a degree in arts the study of Aristotle's *De Anima*. Even the Dominicans—those who had settled in bishoprics in Byzantine lands still under the domination of the western Church—undertook the task of translating directly from the Greek the entire *Metaphysics*. And, from 1240 on, the influence of Aristotle's commentator Averroes had a yet more "subversive" effect. Of all the perils of the new age, most dangerous perhaps was the fascination this kind of philosophy had for the little world of professional thinkers, the men who supplied creative art with its intellectual paradigms. Forming as it did a coherent whole, it had to be accepted (or rejected) *en bloc*. It gave a total, intelligible explanation of the universe and its infinite diversity. At first, then, Aristotelianism had been welcomed as a serviceable instrument, the most efficacious means available for a proper understanding of the scheme of things. The Greek philosopher had proved to be a trusty guide in the exploration of the labyrinth of nature, he had helped to a logical classification of species and genera, assigned each to its due place—in a word had enabled man to draw nearer to the godhead. But closer study of his philosophy revealed the distasteful truth: that it was anti-Christian. Averroes made abundantly clear the appeal of Aristotle's teaching to every thoughtful mind, but at the same time its total incompatibility with all the fundamental tenets of Christian theology.

According to Aristotle there had never been a Creation. From all eternity the movements of existing things had been inherent in God, Prime Mover of the celestial spheres; there had been no beginning of the cosmos in time. He had also ruled out any idea of man's freedom; no unique individual personality or destiny existed, only a human species. Like everything else, a man's body decays and dies; only his rational mind survives, but this spark of being is common to all and, parted from its fleshly shell, becomes submerged in the impersonal. In this bleak and abstract universe the Incarnation and the Redemption could have no place, no meaning. The trouble was that this philosophy commanded respect and as a whole seemed convincing. What hope was there of analysing it out into its elements, dissecting it, then overriding it? Logic, that new weapon given to Catholic dogma by the universities, had defeated Catharism. But how could it defeat Aristotle, when his philosophy relied on the same methods as those which, since the progress made in dialectics, had guided the doctors of the Church and even supplied the scaffolding of their theology? How harmonize this conception of a natural order of things, seemingly inviolable and invariable, with Holy Writ, with the teachings of St Augustine, the movements of efflux and return described by Dionysius? Needless to say, the influence of Aristotle and Averroes seriously affected only a very limited circle. But, as it was, this small circle was composed of the most advanced thinkers of the day, pioneers of the new culture. The younger men, students in the faculty of arts, accepted the new philosophy with neophyte enthusiasm, and there was no holding them. After 1250 the Church's worst enemy was not the Cathar "Perfectus" but the philosopher. Inevitably he became the target of attack. The papacy mobilized against him its militia, the mendicant Orders. It had already censured Joachim of Floris. In the universities it protected Dominicans and Franciscans against the attacks of Guillaume de Saint-Amour. In 1255 Pope Alexander IV ordered Albertus Magnus to refute the errors of Averroes, and three years later he appointed to the two chief chairs of theology in Paris Thomas Aquinas and Bonaventura: a Friar Preacher and a Friar Minor, both Italians.

The face of Jesus in the art of the cathedrals, guided by learned ecclesiastics, bore the stamp of intellect and reason. The populace, however, who no longer found in the old liturgic rites a remedy for their spiritual anxieties and, though more mentally alert than in the past, were still poorly educated and incapable of following the arguments of the professors to their conclusion, pictured to themselves another Christ, more fraternal, less aloof—the historical Christ whom Peter Waldo sought to evoke in his translations of the Gospels, who figured in the sermons of nonconformist preachers, and whom the Crusaders had glimpsed in Palestine. In Byzantium the Christian masses had felt a similar desire much sooner. But the Eastern Church had been untouched by the Gregorian reform. In it clerics and laymen were not so sharply differentiated and its married priests lived in closer contact with their flocks. It was accepted that every believer partook, after his fashion, in the divine illumination and that therefore the Church should countenance all the forms of spirituality that sprang up spontaneously among the population. Long before Roman Christendom, the Eastern Church included in its pastorals the Gospel anecdotes and pictorialized them. True, the figure of the Pantocrator still lorded it in Byzantine apses. And in the frescoes in the Serbian monastery of Mileseva, painted about 1230, the Virgin of the Annunciation, pure, apart and stately—like the Torcello Virgin—has the perfect, other-worldly form of her who was the instrument of God's incarnation. But in another fresco in the monastery we see a very different Mary, weeping on her Son's wounded hand. As at Nerez, fifty years earlier, on the first of the Pietàs.

The West became acquainted with these images, in which the divine was aligned to the human condition, largely as a result of the capture of Constantinople in 1204 and the spoils brought back by the crusaders. But there was an accessory cause: the development of trade routes along the Danube into the heart of southern Germany, whose merchant-adventurers roved the East and whose emperor had closer contacts than any other European monarch with the court of his colleague, the Byzantine emperor. In Swabian missals and psalters and in the Naumburg reliefs, the poignancy of the scenes of the Passion reflects that of the Byzantine Calvaries.

THE DEPOSITION, 13TH CENTURY. POLYCHROME WOOD. VOLTERRA CATHEDRAL.

179

THE BONMONT PSALTER: THE CRUCIFIXION, ABOUT 1260. FOLIO 15 VERSO, MS 54, BIBLIOTHÈQUE MUNICIPALE, BESANÇON.

FRANCISCAN PIETY

Nowhere did Byzantine imagery have more influence than in Italy, where the preaching of St Francis was launching a great religious revival. The Poverello consecrated his life's work to the service of the humblest elements of the population and after his death crowds flocked to his tomb. The memoirs of his disciples, those who had known him in his lifetime, are full of naive anecdotes appealing to the simple folk for whom they were intended. The Fioretti *give us but a vague idea of the features of this uniquely Christlike saint. He figures in some pictures, but we must remember that Berlinghieri and the other Lucca painters did not cater for an élite but for a quite unsophisticated public whose emotions were easily stirred by reminiscences of the saint's life. The defects of these rather childish depictions are redeemed by their evident sincerity.*

At Pisa and other towns of Tuscany large painted wooden effigies of Christ Crucified had been made long before the days of Berlinghieri. They were suspended in churches, above the triumphal arch; their function was to proclaim to the congregation the victory of Christ, and also that of the Church whose face, identical with the Virgin's, was shown in a medallion affixed to the end of the right arm of the cross. But for the poor the crucifix had a different message; the body they saw was that of a man whose precious blood would wash them clean of sin. Had not St Francis, when gazing at one of these crucifixes, seen with his own eyes the Saviour bend towards him with a look of fraternal understanding and heard the divine voice bidding him expound, quite simply, to the people the meaning of His sacrifice and its redemptive power. By the time the rumor went round that St Francis himself had received in his hands and feet the marks of his crucified Saviour, the Tuscan crucifix had ceased to be an emblem of triumph and become one of suffering.

Around 1200 Pisan artists sometimes placed scenes of the Deposition, the Entombment, the Holy Women at the Sepulchre and the Resurrection on either side of the body of the Saviour. It was on His body that Giunta Pisano (active between 1236 and 1254) and Coppo di Marcovaldo (active between 1260 and 1276) focused their emotive effects, and soon in the art of Cimabue the tragedy of the death of God was summed up in an eloquent Crucifixion.

BONAVENTURA BERLINGHIERI (ACTIVE 1228-1274). ST FRANCIS AND SCENES FROM HIS LIFE, 1235.
CHURCH OF SAN FRANCESCO, PESCIA.

CIMABUE (ACTIVE 1272-1302). WOODEN CRUCIFIX, LATE 13TH CENTURY.
MUSEO DELL'OPERA DI SANTA CROCE, FLORENCE.

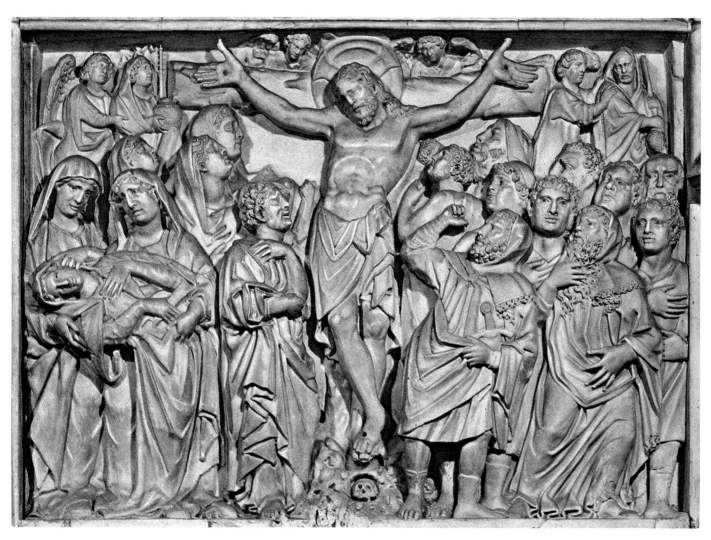

NICOLA PISANO (ABOUT 1220-1278). THE CRUCIFIXION, 1260. DETAIL OF THE MARBLE PULPIT IN THE BAPTISTERY OF PISA.

REVELATION OF ITALY

Between 1250 and 1280 the economic prosperity of Europe made rapid strides, but gradually a change came over its orientation. The first advance, headed by the provinces best equipped for agriculture, was made in rural districts, with the Ile-de-France taking the lead. When its course was deflected to the towns, those in the wealthier provinces awakened from their age-old slumber. But while the great urban centers constantly expanded in the second half of the century, the peasants of northern France had reached the limit of their possibilities. All potentially fertile tracts had been brought under cultivation and no new land was being reclaimed. Here and there, indeed, the cultivators had carried their advance too far, into poor land whose resources were quickly exhausted. Disappointed, they abandoned it, let it run waste again, and there were signs of an agricultural recession. Productivity dropped in many places, since the soil had been overworked and no remedies for this exhaustion, in the way of new techniques, had been discovered. Yet the population went on increasing, and this increase led to a rise in the number of landless peasants who, finding no other employment, worked at starvation rates. The large landlords exploited the situation and, given the abundant supply of cheap labor, could sell their wheat at a handsome profit and so grew ever richer. But, as a corollary, many peasants suffered acutely from poverty and hunger. This overpopulation lay at the root of the widespread unrest, the outbreaks of revolt, and such hare-brained ventures as that of the Pastoureaux and the Children's Crusade. In the regions in which Gothic art was born a startling contrast existed between the state of affairs prevailing in the countryside, afflicted by shortages of food, epidemics and a constant sense of peril, and the towns secure within their walls, hives of ever-increasing activity, where men could eat their fill, drink wine, and money flowed freely. The wealth of the thirteenth century was in the hands of the townsfolk; of money-lenders and patricians who, having bought the estates of spendthrift nobles, squeezed the peasants, their debtors, and lured their sons to the town in order to pay lower wages to their employees. In Paris, in the cloth-making towns of Flanders and in the great markets of Champagne, businessmen made fortunes. The most successful tried to acquire a veneer of culture. Some married dowerless girls of noble birth. They aped the manners of the knights and they, too, patronized poets. For the entertainment of the Arras bankers, song writers and stage producers invented the comic theater. In France, however, at the close of the thirteenth century, the middle class were still relatively uncultured. Not so in Italy, *par excellence* a land of cities.

For some time wealthy traders from the north had been buying south of the Alps their most popular and profitable merchandise: spices, pepper, indigo, and the dainty fabrics sought after by royal princesses and archbishops: silks from Lucca, fine Florentine cloth. Most important of all, Italian mints provided much of the currency needed by commerce. The economic center of France lay in a part of the country where precious metal was still in short supply for purposes of coinage; most of it found its way into cathedral treasures or was converted into the personal adornments of the ruling class. Numbers of men from Asti and Piacenza carrying large moneybags traveled from fair to fair and set up their trestle tables in the marketplace. These Italian moneychangers were at once envied and disliked (as much as Jews), but the prince protected them, since they kept him in funds. In Paris the Lombards had a street of their own near the river; they looked after the royal exchequer and directed the flow of capital in the city. When towards the middle of the century the minting of gold coins was resumed in Europe, most were made in factories at Genoa and Florence.

The fact that certain Italian cities had what was practically a monopoly in this field may well have been an indirect outcome of the crusades, which did so much to stimulate the taste for sea ventures in southern Europe. But it was also a result of the many pilgrimages made to the Holy Land, in the course of which the pilgrim ships put in at flourishing seaports in the eastern Mediterranean, where passengers and crews went on shore and visited the local bazaars, packed with tempting merchandise of all descriptions. In the eleventh century, when so many good Christians of the West had their eyes fixed on Jerusalem, Italian ship-builders were kept busy producing ships to convey the first bands of pilgrims towards the tomb of Christ. These men paid their fares; often they had scraped together the money by selling their estates to monasteries or mortgaging them. Some of this money found its way into the pockets of the shipmen who invested it in local produce, thus opening up commercial dealings with the Near East. Then came the crusade. Its huge armies followed the land route, but for the reconquest of Jerusalem they were helped by the fleets of Pisa and Genoa, which gladly put their shipping at the service of the Knights of Christ. In the thirteenth century most of the crusaders embarked at Pisa, Genoa and Venice on ships that were being constantly improved and built in larger numbers as the eastern trade grew more and more remunerative. Shipwrights and crews were quick to exploit this new source of wealth. The princes in command of the Christian expeditions not only left huge sums in their hands but gave them exclusive trading rights and exemptions from customs duties in the newly Christianized seaports. Sometimes, when the crusaders could not pay their fares in cash, they worked their passage by serving as ordinary seamen. The Venetians brought off the most skillful *coup* of all when, in order to safeguard their commercial privileges, they successfully diverted an entire crusade to Constantinople, richest city in the world, stormed and plundered by the crusaders in 1204.

The inhabitants of the cities from which they hailed supplied the sea-venturers with the capital they needed to open up trade with the Levant. There they speculated in the exchange and bought goods which fetched high prices in the French market. The pope placed an embargo on commercial dealings with the infidels, but they made light of it. Many lost their lives at sea or died of fever, but the others amassed fortunes which they invested, through their business associates, in the transmontane banks. In the mid-thirteenth century the Genoese took to

building larger ships, equipped for longer voyages. In 1251 one of them conveyed to Tunis two hundred passengers and two hundred and fifty tons of freight. Another, in 1277, for the first time doubled the Spanish coast and contacted the ports of Flanders, thus opening up the new sea route which was, later, to spell the end of the great fairs of Champagne, and divert traffic from the commercial highways to which many regions of France still owed their affluence. This change of orientation, which had been gaining ground for two centuries, had ended in 1250 by placing Italian businessmen at the head of the world's economy. And gradually it also committed to their hands the direction of the cultural progress of the West. Thus at the very time when, everywhere else, there still was talk of the transfer of the native habitat of art and philosophy, first from Greece to Rome, then from Rome to Paris, a new mutation was getting under way. So far it was almost imperceptible and had made little obvious progress. For many years to come the university of Paris was to hold its dominant position and no contemporary Italian edifice could vie with Reims Cathedral. Nevertheless the great saint of the thirteenth century was not St Louis, King of France. He was the son of an undistinguished citizen of Assisi.

This upsurge of commerce in the Italian cities gave rise to a new social order. True, the townsfolk had, long before this, succeeded in restricting the clergy to their liturgical functions and in shaking off the domination of the barons. But whereas in French towns the commune was composed exclusively of bourgeois, in Italy it had remained aristocratic, the nobles had controlled it from the start. During the thirteenth century, however, in the new-rich towns, the more active elements of the population began to challenge the power of the nobility and even to usurp it. In any case the class barriers, here, were less restrictive than those elsewhere between the knights and the commonalty. Now these barriers were still further lowered. Many noblemen, perforce or voluntarily, joined commercial firms, took a share in businesses or banks, while would-be patricians of the middle class adopted the way of life of the nobility, built towers on to their houses, bore arms and aspired to joining in the jousts of the knights. St Francis indulged in the recreations of a young nobleman in his early days. Already in 1200, in Italy, successful businessmen were beginning to live up to the standards of the aristocracy.

Such were the material and spiritual conditions under which arose a culture whose singularity became particularly apparent about 1250. One of its most striking characteristics was the cult of poverty, which (after a first brief deviation into heresy) was enthusiastically practised by the followers of St Francis. In the Italian communes, where the priests were less qualified than elsewhere to pose as models of sanctity, the clergy was looked askance at, and most of the cathedral schools stagnated. Thus those desirous of spiritual guidance turned instinctively towards the famous hermits who chanted Matins and Lauds in lonely grottoes, or towards the mendicant friars. Ardent though it was, religion in the towns had a poetic tinge; it was a matter of emotion rather than profound conviction. Intellectual activities found outlets outside the Church, in utilitarian disciplines: the study of law with an eye to the magistracy, or of mathematics, useful for the aspiring businessman. In the Mediterranean coastal towns the sons of merchants learnt Arabic. Some knew it well enough to read Arab manuals of arithmetic. In 1202 Leonardo of Pisa published his *Liber abaci*, which included a treatise on Moslem algebra. In practice these mathematical formulas were used more by accountants than by cathedral builders. For the new culture was slow to find expression in artistic forms congenial to it.

Capital circulated freely. Lent to the king of France and his bishops, it enabled them to build the transmontane cathedrals. But in the Italian cities little was as yet invested in works of art. For "squandering" of this kind was discouraged by the merchant class which now had a voice in municipal affairs, and also by the growing number of believers in a strict interpretation of the Gospel message. Though Dante was soon to trounce the excessive elegance of the Florentines, the amenities of town life in Italy (as everywhere else in Europe) were as yet of an extreme sobriety. For the churches hardly any new adornments were invented; mosaic workers and painters took guidance from Byzantine models; architects and sculptors, from Romanesque prototypes. The few faint stirrings of a new life that little by little modified their accents derived from St Francis and his conception of the holiness of all life. So far ancient Rome was not a source of inspiration; jurists were studying the maxims of Roman legislators, but the poets were little read and the wonders of Roman art still lost to view beneath successive layers of culture deposited by the intervening years, and thickened now by the renewed contacts with the East. Even in Rome herself the pope was a man, trained in Paris, to whose thinking it was the art of France that provided the best formulas for celebrating the power of the Church—and his own. Convinced that the art of the past had erred in glorifying the secular power of the emperors, rivals of the Church, he encouraged the use of the French art forms. This explains why the first resurgence of Roman forms did not take place in the cities of Tuscany or Lombardy, or even in Rome. There was, however, one part of Italy where the imperial power had held its own before succumbing to the attacks of the papacy. This was the kingdom of Sicily.

A little world apart. Could it even be regarded as included in Italy or as a Latin country? For Sicily lay beyond the boundary line which in antiquity had divided the Greek portion of the Empire from the Latin—a division which had been but little altered by the upheavals of the early Middle Ages. Situated at a junction of the newly opened sea routes, Sicily, Calabria, Apulia and Campania were still accessible in 1250 to the influences of all three Mediterranean cultures: Hellenic, Arab and West Christian. For a long while Byzantium had dominated this region. Part of it had been colonized by the Arabs. Then in the mid-eleventh century Norman adventurers had conquered Sicily. Their administrative organization was based on the feudal system, of lords and vassals subject to a royal suzerain, to which they were accustomed. But they were careful to maintain the methods of taxation, the prerogatives and regulations of the despotism they had superseded, and by these means built up the most powerful monarchy in Europe. The Norman rulers gathered round them priests and Latin monks and became the most loyal allies of the popes. None the less, even under the Norman yoke, the population of the island kept to their time-old way of life, their language and traditions. Though their kings kept open house to the troubadours, Greek and Arabic were written and spoken at their court. They followed the advice of Moslem doctors and astrologers. Far more than Regensburg, but also far more than even Antioch (whose rulers as it so happened were Sicilians), far more than the distant outposts of Genoa on the further shore of the Black Sea, more too than Venice, linked though it was with Byzantium, and more even than Toledo, Palermo was a place of curious and fruitful encounters where Westerners could indulge their taste for the exotic to their hearts' content. For there was no question of a few colonies violently implanted here and there in a hostile environment, of strongholds held precariously by bold adventurers, or of those favored cities to which warlike barons retired to take life easy between two successful forays. No, Palermo was the capital of a very ancient State, large and well established, opening with calm self-confidence on all the horizons of the sea. The benefactions of its rulers had enriched Cluny; the kings of Western Europe halted there on journeys back from the Holy Land. They felt at home there, among men who shared their faith and talked in the same way. Even so, this was the East. Like new Theodoras, the Sicilian princesses, scented, dressed in silk, lounged the hours away in sunlit orange groves. An East tuned to western ways, though retaining its peculiar glamour. Members of the royal household translated Hippocrates and Ptolemy into Latin and when, in the twelfth century, monasteries were erected for the Benedictine monks, their Romanesque arcades were promptly covered with a profusion of strange flowers and foliage and the walls submerged in a glittering haze of mosaics or by the decorative carving favored by the Moslem schools of theology.

At the beginning of the thirteenth century Frederick Barbarossa's grandson, when a mere child, succeeded to the throne of Sicily. Twenty-two years later the pope appointed him to the throne of Caesar. However Frederick II, though a Hohenstaufen, was no German, and with him the Holy Roman Empire reverted to the Mediterranean. St Louis, his contemporary and ally, was his cousin, but there could not be a greater contrast than that between these two men. Temperamental, physically a weakling— "in the slave market he would not have fetched two hundred sous"—but versatile and brilliantly intelligent, Frederick was often spoken of as a dangerous man. An implacable enemy of the papacy, several times excommunicated—but what did excommunication mean in those days?—he alone of all the Christian kings had succeeded in reopening to pilgrims the route to Nazareth and Jerusalem. *Stupor mundi et immutator mirabilis* was a contemporary description of this baffling and dynamic ruler, who even in his lifetime seemed a legendary figure. For the Guelfs he was an Antichrist, the beast of the Apocalypse "which rose out of the sea, like unto a leopard; his feet were as the feet of a bear and his mouth as the mouth of a lion, and he opened his mouth in blasphemy against God." The Ghibellines, however, saw in him the emperor of the end of time, and we can sense Dante's regret at having to place him in his Inferno. A legend grew up after his death that he still was sitting in a cavern in the Kyffhäuser mountain, before a stone table through which his beard had grown, waiting for the destined day when the need of his country should call him forth to restore to the Empire at long last a golden age of prosperity and peace.

Writing a hundred years after Frederick's death, Villani, the Florentine chronicler, described him thus. "A man of mark and sterling worth, of natural ability and all-embracing knowledge. He knew the Latin language, Italian, German, French, Greek and Arabic; was richly endowed with all virtues, liberal and courteous in giving, valiant and skilled in arms, and feared exceedingly. But he was dissolute and voluptuous, and had many concubines and mamelukes, after the Saracenic fashion. For he was addicted to sensual pleasures and led an Epicurean life, never giving a thought to any other life. He and his sons reigned in great glory but, for their sins, fell on evil days, and their lineage died out." True, Frederick II was an incorrigible amorist, but so were all the princes of the age—with the exception of St Louis. True, too, he had his chancellor's eyes put out, but there was no sadistic intent. Deriving from Byzantium, it was an accepted form of punishment in that part of Europe. He fraternized with infidels and his fortress at Lucera was garrisoned by Moors; he called Malik al-Kamil, Sultan of Egypt, his friend, exchanged gifts with him, and even knighted Moslem ambassadors. But there was no question here of unbelief or even lukewarmness; on the contrary his faith was absolute. He did not smile when leading the crusade. But he had an inquiring mind and liked having the God of the Jews and Mohammad's Allah explained to him. Just as one day he wanted to have a talk with St Francis. For the rest, he hounded heretics down ruthlessly, supported the Inquisition more strenuously than any other monarch of the age, and on his deathbed had himself clad in the Cistercian habit. A mass of contradictions, the Emperor seemed almost incomprehensible to the thirteenth-century theologians and chroniclers, whose minds were all of a piece. But then Frederick was a Sicilian.

More to the point for our present purpose is his thirst for knowledge. A knowledge somewhat different no doubt from that of the Parisian theologians. It stemmed not only from Aristotle, but from other books translated at the emperor's expense from Greek and Arabic. From personal experience, too; Frederick himself wrote a treatise on venery in which he minutely described the animals he hunted. The story went that one day he made a man die in an hermetically sealed jar so as to discover what became of the soul after death. For southern Italy was in the nature of a special case in the domain of scientific culture. In virtue of its prelates and inquisitors it belonged to the Catholic world and from its lawyers, trained in the schools of Bologna, it had learnt the disciplines of scholastic logic. All the same Euclid, Averroes and the accumulated wisdom of Greece and Islam were not like foreign bodies in Sicilian culture, but of a piece with it. The king presided at debates conforming, as at Oxford and Paris, to the strict rules of dialectics, setting forth the questions at issue and the conclusions arrived at. Problems of algebra, medicine and astrology were discussed at these reunions. Like the sultans, anxious to discover what the future had in store for him, Frederick consulted alchemists, mages, necromancers and horoscope casters, and in a Faustian desire to solve the riddle of existence steeped himself in the lore of Oriental occultism. Peter of Eboli, author of the *De Rebus Siculis Carmen*, composed for him a poem on the nature of the waters of Pozzuoli and their virtues; his shoeing-smith made for him a manual of farriery, and his astrologer brought back from Toledo Al-Bitruji's *Astronomy* and Aristotle's writings on zoology.

The Emperor and the savants at his court brought to the observation of natural phenomena the same lucidity as the Parisian masters. They were not, however, so much obsessed with a desire to orient their analysis of the created world towards its divine Maker; their physics was not tinctured with theology, but was a secular, autonomous discipline. Not that there was any doubt of their belief in the divinity of Christ and the efficacy of the sacraments. They regarded as "sinners" Aristotle, Averroes and all the Saracen or Jewish teachers who instructed them, looked after their bodies, read the stars for them. But their religion, like that of the towns of Tuscany, had something of the quality of poetry; it did not wholly dominate their intellectual researches

or their probings into the mysteries of the visible world. When Reims and Chartres were being built the South Italians observed a cautious attitude towards the dogmas given visible embodiment in the cathedrals. Interested above all in reality, they applied themselves to detecting the forces at work in the growth of plants, the behavior of animals and the movements of the stars. In a purely detached manner, as in the schools of Islam. Perhaps because they tended to disregard the significance of the Incarnation and attributed to God the transcendence of the Moslem Allah, placing Him at an immeasurably far remove from the material world. This, anyhow, was the attitude prevailing in Frederick's entourage where for the first time in Christendom there arose a purely physical science unconcerned with the divine. Here that lively sense of concrete actuality developed which, a century and a half later, was to be reflected in the art of the Italian cities. This realism, so different from the realism of the Gothic cathedrals, owed its origin not (as is sometimes thought) to a new spirit awaking in the middle class, but to the direct encouragement of a king of whom it was said in the courts of Europe that he "lived like a sultan."

Along with St Louis this monarch was the greatest art patron of the period. When, after being chosen German king in 1218, Frederick II was crowned emperor two years later, he ordered his artists to break with the Byzantine traditions of his Palermitan ancestors. On his father's side he was a Swabian and he was backed by the Order of Teutonic Knights. Since an imperial art was what he wanted, he discouraged any sort of adaptation of the arts of France, which celebrated the glories of the Capetian kings and found favor with the Holy See. He preferred to patronize art forms that had recently sprung up on imperial soil, at Lucca and Modena: forms whose origins lay far away, in the primeval forests of Ottonian Germany. It was in the early years of his reign that the aesthetic of Lombardy succeeded in establishing itself in southern Italy. Figuring in the guise of a donor, the emperor had himself given the features of a Romanesque "idol" at Bitonto, and the columns of the royal basilica of Altamura carried zoomorphic capitals like those of Parma. But the young emperor took stock little by little of the prerogatives with which his coronation in 1220 had invested him. He heard much talk in royal circles of the might of "Caesar light of the world" and was attended by jurists who based their arguments on Justinian's Codex. When his troops had crushed the militias of the Lombard league, he had the trophies of his victory carried in triumph to the Capitol. His next step was to resuscitate the Roman eagles and fasces. The art of the bishops of Tuscany and Emilia could no longer celebrate his virtues now that he had ousted the papacy from Rome. Of a purely military and temporal order, his sovereignty had no need of religious rites. After 1233 he built no more churches; only castles, symbols of his might. Given an octagonal form, like the Carolingian chapel at Aix-la-Chapelle, Castel del Monte represents the imperial crown and at the same time the heavenly Jerusalem. But its eight walls—image of eternity in the mystique of numbers—did not shelter sacred relics or a chapter of canons intoning the liturgy. They demonstrated for all to see the might of the Christian Caesar, God's viceregent on earth, and in the decorative scheme the elegant precision of the art of Champagne replaced the visionary splendors of Romanesque. At the very time when St Louis was starting to build the Sainte-Chapelle, in homage to the Christ of the Gothic "coronations," Frederick had a statue of himself, as Caesar Augustus, erected at Capua. Thus ancient Rome was resuscitated, superb and victorious, from the dead past.

A short-lived reincarnation. In 1250 the great emperor died, and with him the grandiose reality of the Empire. Contemporaries saw in this collapse of the "imperial idea" one of the most striking indications of the dawn of a new age. Frederick's line died out. But Charles of Anjou, brother of St Louis, who, supported by the papacy, supplanted Frederick's offspring on the throne of Sicily, did not wholly obliterate the unique cultural flowering whose seeds had been sown in the island by the Hohenstaufen king and which the driving force of thirteenth-century Italy had brought to fruition. This prince, whose emblem was the *fleur de lys*, espoused all the ambitions of his predecessors, the Norman kings of Palermo, and their dreams of conquest on the three shores of the Mediterranean. He did not expel from his court the astrologers, physicians and translators. Peter of Maricourt, his "master of experiments," made astrolabes for him and soon his effigy in stone, invested with all the ponderous majesty of the Roman statues, lorded it in a public place. Charles wished to be acclaimed as a man of learning and a scientist, like his "opposite number" oversea, Alfonso the Learned, King of Castile, author of manuals of astronomy. So it was that the sculptors of Campania continued to borrow from ancient sarcophagi effigies of a majesty other than religious and these won general admiration. Indeed in central Italy they were felt to be better suited to the spirit of the time than were Byzantine or Romanesque symbols or the art forms of France. The decoration of Amiens Cathedral was still uncompleted when at Pisa Nicola Pisano carved the pulpit of the baptistery. Thus in an age of crisis and confusion the art of a new era took its rise at the southern extremity of Europe, on a soil prepared for it by Frederick II.

6

RESURRECTION OF ROME

It may seem strange that thirteenth-century Italy, despite the spectacular upsurge of prosperity that was soon to give it the lead on the economic plane of all the nations of Europe, failed to produce any works of art comparable to those of Chartres, Reims or Bamberg. The reason was that Italy did not constitute a State, but was divided into a great many autonomous political units. No sovereign concentrated in his hands the power of exploiting all the wealth of the country, no Italian court could vie with that of the king of France or even that of the king of Germany. Here the authority which in the past had enabled the monarch to promote the building and guide the destinies of the great cathedrals and monastic churches, had disintegrated. Established in Rome, the Pope claimed to govern the whole of Christendom, but the power he wielded was essentially spiritual; he had not as yet the fiscal machinery needed to fill his coffers, or funds for artistic ventures as prodigal and prodigious as those of St Louis. Theoretically all the central part of the peninsula was under his direct rule, but the pontifical agents were hampered by local town authorities and by the feudal nobility who, secure in their strongholds, flouted the Holy See. Similarly, the former ascendancy of the Lombard kings had lost much of its force, once they had become entangled with the kings of Germany over the claims the latter made for their "rights" in Tuscany and the Po valley—always in vain. For again and again when the German cavalry swept down through the Brenner, all they succeeded in extracting from the towns was a semblance of surrender. The Italians gave way for a moment, then waited for the plague and fever to decimate the Teutonic army and for its leader to beat an ignominious retreat, empty-handed. The communes in Lombardy and the valley of the Arno retained their independence, but their wealth was now split up, in small parcels, among a number of warring republics.

There was then only one well-established State in Italy, capable of financing large-scale enterprises, and that was the Kingdom ruled by the Princes of Palermo. They amassed enormous wealth and spent it freely on adorning their residences and churches. But the provinces they governed formed part of the eastern world, and it was Greek artists they called in to decorate with glittering mosaics their banquet halls and places of worship.

However, a radical change came over southern Italy when Sicily became incorporated in the Hohenstaufen heritage and Frederick II, once he had come of age, resolved to prove himself a worthy successor of the Caesars. This political change gave rise, in the only Italian court where there was scope for largesse on a truly regal scale, to a complete reversal of the then prevailing aesthetic, a return to Roman sources and the restoration, under the guidance of archaeologists, of classical art. Throughout the thirteenth century fantastic animals, dragons, hippocampi, deriving from Byzantine textiles, had wound their way into the ambos of cathedrals. The new art did not expel them, nor did it invade the churches; to begin with it was limited to civic monuments. Long before this, in the Lombard provinces, Romanesque aesthetic had struck root down to the deepest stratum, that of Roman antiquity. It excluded both the all-pervasive light and the vital impulse of the new French cathedrals. Like the ancient temples, the Romanesque church was shut-in, girdled with arcadings, and stability was the architect's prime concern. The Parma Baptistery rises skywards, but in the form of a cylinder, not a spire, and the statues ornamenting it have a family likeness to those of the gods and deified heroes on the gates of Latin cities, on their mausolea and

triumphal arches. But it was under the aegis of Frederick II that Roman statuary was systematically resuscitated.

The castle of Capua, built between 1234 and 1240—the years which witnessed the apogee of the statuary at Reims and Bamberg—contains some remarkable busts in which we see a reversion to Antiquity pure and simple, ungarbled by the liturgical allusions dear to the Romanesque sculptors. Indeed these effigies of the Emperor, of his counsellors, and of the civic virtues, might well have been brought to light by excavations on some ancient site. Soon they were copied by the decorators of religious edifices. In 1272, in Ravello Cathedral, the sculptor Nicola di Bartolomeo da Foggia, whose father had been employed by Frederick II, included a woman's head in the decoration of the bishop's throne. Was this a portrait of Sigilgaida Rufolo as some have thought? More probably an allegory of the Church; for in this face we surely have the visage of ancient Rome herself, reborn.

For some time the large cities of Tuscany had equalled in wealth the greatest princes of the land; but their citizens were then engaged in a struggle with the aristocracy, whose power they were gradually undermining. The leaders of the communes, who were in charge of the finances of these cities, were for the most part businessmen who had recently risen from the ranks and whose culture was only superficial. Still, some of them had taste and sense enough to purchase abroad (as did some New York bankers and Muscovite financiers at the turn of the last century) the finest extant works of art. But these were Byzantine ornaments and French illuminated books. These new men were well aware that the craftsmen of the Tuscan towns lacked both the imagination and the skill needed for creating the type of works on which their heart was set. Then Nicola Pisano came on the scene. Little is known of him except that he was born about 1220 and died in 1278. His statues (in stone) of Moses show the Lawgiver descending not from Sinai but the heights of Olympus. It was in 1260, year of the completion of Reims Cathedral, also the very year which according to Joachim of Floris was to usher in the Third Age of the world, that Nicola carved the famous Pisan pulpit, heralding the "new birth" of plastic art.

RESURRECTION OF ROME

1. Bust of the Emperor Frederick II. Mid-13th century. Museo Civico, Barletta.

2. View of Castel del Monte (Apulia), built by Frederick II in 1240.

3. Three pages from an illustrated manuscript of Frederick II's treatise on falconry *(De arte venandi cum avibus)*. 1220-1250. Vatican Library.

4. Base of a pulpit or paschal candlestick with four male figures. Emilia, 13th century. Museo Civico, Bologna.

5. Nicola di Bartolomeo da Foggia. Portrait bust of Sigilgaida Rufolo (?). 1272. Marble. Ravello Cathedral.

6. Bust of Pietro della Vigna, minister of Frederick II. 1239. Museo Campano, Capua.

7. Marble pulpit with mosaic decorations by Nicola di Bartolomeo da Foggia. 1272. Ravello Cathedral.

6

7

HAPPINESS

After the middle of the century the inventive powers of the artists employed on the French cathedrals began to flag. They made use of methods ever more logical, ever better calculated to flood the edifice with light, but these procedures were being drained more and more of their spiritual content. One of the reasons for this gradual despiritualization was the change in the system of education. The university devoted its energies almost exclusively to improvements in the mechanism of dialectics, and true culture was the loser in this process. The young men turned out by the schools were experts in the technique of reasoning and little else. Another reason was that fewer prelates took any real interest in creative art. More and more of them belonged to the mendicant Orders and many were of humble extraction. "Son of a churl and wife no better!" Thus Joinville described the Franciscan Robert de Sorbon who was annoying him, and went on to call him "a traitor to the candor of his forefathers." A good many of these prelates who, by way of the episcopate, had achieved the highest social rank became dazzled by their new eminence, addicted to luxurious living, and when it came to cathedral building interested chiefly in architectural *tours de force* and finished execution. The best of the clergy, those who kept faith with the spirit of poverty, were more concerned with preaching than with building, and when they struck out on new paths these led towards an ever greater humility, a more wholehearted devotion to the lesson of the Master. Monumental form meant little to them. St Bonaventura did not build cathedrals, he left that to the king of France, a truly saintly man, but not a professed theologian. So little by little the control of creative architecture passed into the hands of specialists, the "master-masons."

The status of these men had risen far above that of the artisans whose work they supervised. They were no longer expected, as in earlier times, to lend a hand in carrying stones or to carve these stones themselves. Experts in measurement, they submitted to the chapter a carefully worked out elevation, on parchment, of the projected edifice. "Some men," as a preacher of the time observed, "work with words. In the building of these large edifices there is commonly someone in charge who gives the others their orders by word of mouth and seldom or never stirs a finger. Compass and foot-rule in hand the master-mason tells his men, 'Make a cut here.' And though he does not do the work, he gets the highest wages." The master-masons knew all the secrets of their craft and were on easy terms with the doctors of the university who initiated them into the "science of numbers" and the lore of dialectics. But these men were not priests, they did not consecrate Christ's body, they had not spent long hours meditating on the Word of God and wrestling with its obscurities. They were executants, they did not draw inspiration, as Suger and Maurice de Sully had done, from a contemplation of the divine hierarchies, but applied themselves to solving problems of stresses and stability. When it came to invention, their approach was that of the technician, not the mystic; their business was that of handling raw material to best effect, not of elucidating mysteries. Those with a logical turn of mind gauged their success in terms of strict geometry. There were, however, some more sensitive practitioners whose ideal was not so much truth as beauty.

At Saint-Denis, around 1250, that great architect Peter of Montreuil did not innovate; he refined on what had been done before. He had a gift for exploiting to the full the aesthetic possibilities of an edifice; for arranging the disposition of light with a view to the pleasure of the eye as well as for homiletic ends. The two rose windows of the transept, one of them with its light converging centrally, the other radiating out in all directions, still conform—thanks to a strictly calculated mathematical formula—to that concept of a dual movement of efflux and return which, originated by Dionysius, was taken over by St Thomas Aquinas. But the careful balance between structure and ornamentation no longer exists. The functional values of the architectural masses are masked and elegance is Peter's prime concern. Similarly, though the statues in the Sainte-Chapelle are exquisitely proportioned they have lost their souls; superficially they resemble the Reims statues, but all the spirituality has gone out of them. When Gaucher, last of the great masters-of-works, installed in the portal the tall carved figures that had been made for it, he discarded the arrangement originally planned, guided by a purely doctrinal purpose. This meaningful arrangement, devised by theologians, seemed to him unsatisfactory. He placed each statue with an eye to its plastic values, no longer to its significance. The canons accepted his rearrangement, for they, too, were coming to like the new aesthetic. Already in the statue personifying the Synagogue the full weight of the body had rested on a single leg and there were intimations of that sinuous movement of the hips which gives fourteenth-century figures of the Virgin and female saints something of the lithe grace of dancers at the princely courts. This medieval "sway" can also be seen in the miniatures of illuminated manuscripts and in the stained-glass windows, where the elegance of the line evidences a desire to please the eye. Thus the Christian masses and the priests, their mentors, took to finding "beautiful" both the Living God and His Mother. This trend towards aestheticism may well have owed something to the crisis theological thought was undergoing in Paris, and to the underground movements that had occasioned it. At the bidding of the pope, St Thomas Aquinas and St Bonaventura led the campaign against the new deviations. The former took his stand on reasoning, entered the lists against Aristotle and his commentator, and set out to rout them in a dialectical tournament. But his Franciscan colleague saw in logic only a means for clearing the ground. "Philosophy is but a path to other forms of knowledge. He who lingers on it remains in darkness." Harking back to St Augustine, he distinguishes the empirical knowledge acquired through the senses, which only perceive appearances, from that deeper understanding which apprehends the glories of the world to come. His *Itinerarium Mentis ad Deum* sets forth the Christian's progress towards ecstatic union with the divine in an intense, all-consuming love. Why, then, waste time arguing with Aristotle? It is far better surely to advance along the path leading to the celestial heights. He warns the "intellectual" of his limitations. "Beware of thinking that you comprehend the incomprehensible." This teaching harmonized better than that of Aquinas with the spirit of the age, and had a direct appeal for those simple believers who in their quest of God trusted instinctively to the guidance of the Spirit. Hence Bonaventura's victory over Thomism, whose premises he controverted in his *Discourses on the Gifts of the Holy Spirit.* In 1270, alarmed by the extravagant claims of dialectics and mindful of the religious feelings of the masses, Catholic theologians deliberately entered on the path of mysticism.

But the mental climate of the Ile-de-France, of Paris prospering greatly in the reign of Philip the Bold, of the intelligentsia at the university and of the nobility, all for elegance and courtly manners, was little suited to any sort of mysticism. The religious zeal which had launched heavenwards the spires of Laon, Chartres and Reims had spent its force in the second half of the thirteenth century; it was shifting eastwards, towards the Rhine valley and the region in which small unorthodox communities such as the Beguines and Beghards were beginning to flourish. Commerce was thriving in Germany, new trade routes were being opened up, forests cut down to make room for towns. Albertus Magnus had left Paris shortly before 1250 and been given the post of lecturer at Cologne, where he expounded the Dionysian hierarchies and was the pride of the new Dominican study center. After him, another Dominican, Ulrich of Strasbourg, amplified and stressed that portion of his teaching which subordinated the techniques of rationalism to the mystique of illumination, thus blazing the trail for that first great speculative mystic, Meister Eckhart. It was the Germany of the Brethren of the Free Spirit and the Minnesingers that inherited the art of the cathedrals, and at Strasbourg that the last great Gothic workyards came into operation. The sculpture of Reims had a remoter offshoot at Naumburg in the heart of a world so far little touched by culture. Here, however, the artists, while taking much from Reims, tended towards expressionism; alongside scenes of the Passion, they set up statues of princesses in the flower of their beauty. In these backwoods, in an environment of visionary monks, the art of France lost much of its lucidity. It was invaded by a horde of monsters from the early Romanesque bestiaries, plunged into a world of phantasms and blind, irrational forces, peopled with those restless or oddly mannered forms into which Byzantine models had been transmuted by their Germanic imitators. Stripped of its logical premises, Suger's clear-cut aesthetic was dissipated in a haze of shimmering light and vague effusions centering on the cult of Mary. It was, in short, adapted to the taste of men who sought in emotion rather than in reflection an anodyne for their spiritual unrest.

In Paris the schoolmen were turning towards another path, still that of reason, but leading to happiness of a terrestrial order. Parisian intellectuals claimed more ardently than ever the right to philosophize and found encouragement in the new trend of theology towards mysticism. Since Christ came on earth and suffered for the salvation of all mankind and since all that the Christian needs for access to celestial joys is a full surrender to His all-embracing love, why should there be a ban on free discussion of secular matters and why deprive oneself of the pleasures of this world? The lay professors in the Faculty of Arts did not take part in theological debates; their task was limited to expounding Aristotle and their lectures on him were addressed to young students many of whom were to follow lay careers. They declared that the faculty of thought, of thinking freely, was essential to the dignity of man; that philosophy was the noblest discipline of all, and pointed the way to the supreme good. Was not its function the discovery of the laws of Nature, the true order of the scheme of things and, since Nature is the work of God, His instrument, a reflection of His mind and the work of His hands, how can it possibly be evil? By carefully exploring its secrets we discover the rule of a perfect life, in accordance with the divine plan. "Sin is in man, but righteous ways spring from the order of Nature. Therefore if man faithfully conforms to this order, he can be sure of pleasing God. And as a reward, he will live a well-balanced and joyous life on earth" (Boethius of Dacia). Thus the new school of thought showed the way to happiness.

A happiness which is the work of man alone and attainable by dint of his intelligence. For Lady Nature offers those who serve her well the gift of perfect bliss even in this earthbound life. That is the lesson of the second *Roman de la Rose* written about 1275 by Jean de Meung, an alumnus of the university of Paris. He denounces the many abuses that have tended to pervert the divine scheme: the lust for power, the meretricious arts of *courtoisie*, the hypocritical preaching of the mendicant friars. Then he evokes the perfect order of the primeval world. "Long ago, in the days of our remote forefathers, men and women, as the Ancients tell us, loved each other with a pure, abiding love, unsullied by gross desire or any sordid motive, and happiness reigned everywhere. Then land was not cultivated but left as God bedecked it; yet every man got from it all he needed." But now God's order had been ruined by Deceit, Pride and Double-dealing.

These ideas may be traced back to Averroes, but they also derived (and more directly) from the anti-heretical propaganda which, to confute the Cathars, insisted on the goodness of the created world. We can see these ideas in the iconography of the Creation figured forth in the art of the cathedrals. Nor did they conflict with that naive optimism of the early phase of Franciscanism which the Holy See, scenting danger, had forced the Minorites to abandon. They also harmonized with the common belief in an approaching millennium and with the aspirations of the underprivileged masses, who had been given to understand that God had created all his children equal. Thus the philosophy in vogue in Paris around 1270 may be regarded as a new phase in the progressive "discovery" of the Incarnation. A decisive forward step; it meant that the religious thought of the schools ceased to be esoteric, reserved to Initiates, and became accessible to laymen.

For, freed as it was from clerical restraints, this proposition of material happiness (the *Roman de la Rose* was written in the language of the courts) appealed to all the knights in love with life and their ladies, and to those who had refused to accompany Louis on his last crusade. ("There was no crusade in those times; none left his native land to go forth and explore foreign countries.") The joyousness of the courtly poems was transposed into another key. Men were invited to open their eyes to the beauty of all creatures and to rejoice in it. This new spirit found expression in the childish laughter of the Elect at Bamberg, in Rutebeuf's witty satires, and in the charming songs composed by the trouvère Adam de la Halle, simpler and more spontaneous than the scholastic polyphony of Pérotin le Grand. This had been the spirit of St Louis in his youth—before he had forgotten how to laugh. And it now lay behind the smiling anti-clericalism of the nobles of the French court and that of an entire generation of healthy-minded, clear-eyed young men for whom the false prophets, precursors of the Last Day, were not the dialecticians of the schools or the troubadours, but the preachers of repentance, canting bigots, who barred the way to the blithe freedom of a new golden age. The younger sculptors, all for grace and beauty, joined forces with them. It was they who provided the rich sap that fed the luxuriant flowers and foliage of the last capitals. And in the Bourges *Resurrection* it is a call to happiness, a glad tomorrow, that has summoned forth the women from their graves, their bodies invested with the grace of youth renewed. At Bourges we see the triumphant expression of that feeling for warm-blooded, truly human beauty which seemed to have died out in Paris in the art of Notre-Dame.

This philosophy of happiness was the outcome of three centuries of uninterrupted progress in the Ile-de-France. In Italy, that land of successful businessmen, it naturally enough was welcomed. But was there not a risk that in a country like Italy, where the ecclesiastical structure was less firmly established, Christianity might disintegrate completely and give place to paganism? Already Frederick II had been charged with impiety of this order. Benvenuto of Imola had this in mind when he said that "soon there were over a hundred thousand men of high estate who believed, like Farinata degli Uberti and Epicurus, that paradise must be sought for in this world and in this world alone." When Dante in the *Inferno* visited the circle to which were relegated

> Along with Epicurus all his followers
> Who hold that the soul dies with the body

it was Farinata who told him

> "With more than a thousand here I lie
> "And herewithin lies Frederick the Second."

Yet it was in his *Paradiso* that Dante placed "the eternal light" of Siger de Brabant, one of the leading Parisian philosophers and a moving spirit of the new school. In his description of the Orders of the world he ranges in two sequences, side by side but separate (as the masters of the Faculty of Arts had done), Church and State, Grace and Nature, Theology and Philosophy. He expressly declares the excellence and the autonomy of Philosophy—*Filosofia è uno amoroso uso di sapienza*—since it shows us

> After what manner Nature takes her course
> From the Intellect Divine and from its art.
> And if thy physics well thou studiest
> After a few pages thou shalt find
> That this thy art, so far as may be,
> Followeth Nature, as the disciple doth his master,
> So that thy art is, as it were, God's grandchild.

We might well regard the *Divine Comedy* as a cathedral, last of the great cathedrals. Dante based it on what he had learnt of scholastic theology from Dominican preachers at Florence who had studied at the university of Paris. For like the French cathedrals the poem leads us upward and onward by gradual degrees, corresponding to the hierarchies of light described by Dionysius, and through the intercession of St Bernard, St Francis and the Virgin, to the love "which moves the stars." Inspired by the Incarnation, the art of the great cathedrals had celebrated to wonderful effect the Body of Christ. That is to say the Church triumphant, the Church invested with worldwide dominion. But at the dawn of the Trecento, a tendency was developing in the western world to free the mind of man from the thrall of priestdom and to deflect his thoughts from the supramundane. Henceforth they were oriented in a different direction, towards "Nature, the art of God" (*Paradiso*, VIII). An art that could but point the way to happiness. Even Dante and his earliest disciples were conscious of this and set their course to a new bourne.

THE ROSE WINDOW

The art of the glass-worker was brought to perfection in the large rose windows which in the mid-thirteenth century were set up over the new transepts. These elaborate compositions signify at once the cycles of the cosmos, the merging of Time into Eternity, and the mystery of a God who is Light, of Christ the sun. Surrounded by apostles, prophets and saints, God is shown in the south rose of Notre-Dame in Paris and He shines forth in the midst of the music-making elders of the Apocalypse in the rose of the Sainte-Chapelle. The Virgin, i.e. the Church, figures in some rose windows. Circular, they demonstrate, in a whirl of rotating spheres, the identity of Aristotle's concentric universe with the centrifugal effusion described by Robert Grosseteste. The rose is also a symbol of love; it represents the fiery core of that divine love in which all human loves are consumed. And we also see in it a figuration of the labyrinth through which profane love gropes its way towards that sacred love which is its goal.

When around 1240 Guillaume de Lorris versified the courtly way of life in a poem embodying "the whole art of love," he named it Le Roman de la Rose. *The rose for him is the ideal lady, the flower the perfect knight passionately yearns to pluck. This he succeeded in doing in Jean de Meung's lengthy continuation of the poem, written some forty years later. Here the allegories are stripped of courtly affectation and given a natural, everyday presentment. Conscious of the cyclical recurrence of life, the ineluctable finality of individual death counterbalanced by the survival of the species, generation after generation, the poet sees in man's love of woman (that desire whose symbol is the rose) an elemental value poles apart from the love-play of the courts of chivalry. In this poem all those trivial, factitious graces are eliminated, man and woman join in a union that is simple, healthy, fecund. Thus the rose becomes an image of victory over death. A victory of Nature, that is to say of God, but also of mankind since all men co-operate in His creative plan. This will to life and the joy of living find superlative expression in the luminous polychromy of the rose window.*

ROSE WINDOW OF THE SOUTH TRANSEPT, WITH THE TRIUMPH OF CHRIST AND THE APOSTLES. ABOUT 1270.
CATHEDRAL OF NOTRE-DAME, PARIS.

JOYS OF LIFE

In the early thirteenth century the lords and ladies of the Ile-de-France were coming to appreciate the elaborate rules of courtly love-making and to find in them a fillip to their pleasures. For them was written the first Roman de la Rose. *However, the world of the courts still was organized in terms of lineage and feudal rights. This is why the knights and their kinsmen the canons never pictured the Virgin in the likeness of one of the damsels of the "garden of love," but as a mother and a great lady. There were of course frequent exchanges in this period between Marian poetry and courtly poetry, each contributing something to the other. But the progress of the cult of Our Lady and the simultaneous rise in prestige of the woman of high birth were separate phenomena; they did not follow the same rhythm, varied from province to province, stemmed from different levels of consciousness and answered to different urges. The image of Mary stood for a mysterious union of the values of virginity, fecundity and royalty that had no place in courtly love, anyhow in its early phase. On the Virgin all the primitive beliefs that had lingered on among the peasantry converged: beliefs that wavered between an atavistic dread of the Mother Goddesses of paganism and an equally superstitious veneration of the sacrosanct objects made by goldsmiths in which, in many monasteries, the relics of patron saints were enshrined. Until, about 1250, a Parisian master for the first time represented the Mother standing, with the Child in her arms, in a graceful attitude, with a slight sway of the hips—that of the figurations of the Church (with which Catholic theology was more and more identifying Mary)—the Gothic Virgin had always been shown in majesty, seated on a throne. This slightly mannered attitude was the one adopted by the wife of the lord at court ceremonies: the woman who had borne in her womb the hope of the line and the future of the House.*

But when the age of the great cathedrals was drawing to a close, a change took place, men's eyes were opening to the beauty of a perfect body, and sculptors began celebrating in large free-standing statues this new-won joy in life. It found elegant expression in the smiling angels of Reims, in a host of wooden angels, their brothers, and in the gracious body of the youthful Adam. It is now that statues of princesses make their first appearance: Yolande of Castile at Burgos, Uta at Naumburg. A habit had long prevailed among the populace of likening that very noble lady, their lord's wife, to the Queen of Sheba. And in Notre-Dame of Paris when the Virgin with the Child rises from her throne she becomes truly Queen of France. Sublimated like the august figures on the tombs, she embodies a perfection existent from all eternity in the mind of God. What she shows the world is still the ideal type-form of sovereignty, but with the added charm of a very lovely woman.

ANGEL. LAST THIRD OF THE 13TH CENTURY. WOOD CARVING FROM CHAMPAGNE. LOUVRE, PARIS.

"THE KNIGHT OF BAMBERG," ABOUT 1235. BAMBERG CATHEDRAL.

213

INDEX OF NAMES

LIST OF ILLUSTRATIONS